200

Low-Carb, High-Fat Recipes

© 2015 Fair Winds Press

First published in the USA in 2015 by
Fair Winds Press, a member of
Quarto Publishing Group USA Inc.
100 Cummings Center, Suite 406-L
Beverly, MA 01915-6101
www.fairwindspress.com
Visit www.QuarrySPOON.com and help us celebrate food and
culture one spoonful at a time!

18 17 16 15   6 7 8 9 10

ISBN: 978-59233-638-8

Digital edition published in 2015
eISBN: 978-1-62788-182-1

Library of Congress Cataloging-in-Publication Data

Carpender, Dana.
  200 low-carb, high-fat recipes : easy recipes to jumpstart your low-carb
weight loss / Dana Carpender.
     pages cm
  ISBN 978-1-59233-638-8 (paperback) — ISBN 978-1-62788-182-1 (eISBN)
 1. Low-carbohydrate diet. 2. Low-carbohydrate diet--Recipes. I. Title. II.
Title: Two hundred low-carb, high-fat recipes.
  RM237.73.C368 2014
  641.5'6383--dc23
                    2014017444

Cover design and book design by Laura H. Couallier,
Laura Herrmann Design

Printed and bound in the United States

200 Low-Carb, High-Fat Recipes

Easy Recipes to Jumpstart your Low-Carb Weight Loss

DANA CARPENDER

Fair Winds Press
100 Cummings Center, Suite 406L
Beverly, MA 01915

fairwindspress.com • quarryspoon.com

This one is for all my pals on the annual Low-Carb Cruise. It's the highlight of my year, truly, and it's because you guys are so, so amazing, astonishing, awe-inspiring, and just plain fun.

For my recipe testers, who once again have done yeoman service. Thanks, all of you—you're the best!

And, of course, to Eric Schmitz, That Nice Boy I Married, without whom this stuff wouldn't get done.

CONTENTS

FOREWORD

Like many people I meet, Dana's entrée into the low-carb lifestyle began from personal experience. The low-fat diet she had been advised to follow wasn't working—and her health reflected it. After years of struggling she ditched the then conventional wisdom and adopted a low-carb diet, lost 45 pounds, dramatically improved her health, and never looked back.

I'll never forget meeting Dana on my first Low Carb Cruise. The Low Carb Cruise is an Annual event which brings together 200–300 low carb enthusiasts (one could say, "zealots") from around the world to learn about low-carbohydrate research and practical advice about living the lifestyle. Once you meet Dana, I doubt that you will ever forget her direct, "just the facts, Ma'am," style. She tells it like she sees it—which makes her cookbooks treasures of practical information. I am grateful to Dana for her prior cookbooks—they have enabled me, my family, and my patients to incorporate healthy low-carb food into our lifestyles.

Why is a clinical research physician and obesity medicine specialist writing a foreword for a cookbook? Because what you eat really matters for your health. I am continually amazed that just by helping people to understand how their bodies respond to what they eat, I can reverse obesity, diabetes, and many other many medical conditions that I used to prescribe medications for as an internal medicine specialist. I can treat, and also prevent, these conditions just by giving advice about how to change the food someone eats. So simple—yet so powerful.

As of 2014, the science supports the low-carb, high-fat lifestyle as a healthy way of eating. From my research and clinical practice, I have come to understand that most people's bodies run better using fat as a fuel instead of carbohydrate (sugars and starches). When you burn fat as your primary fuel—and you can do this by eating fat and protein, and low amounts of carbohydrate—your body's metabolism generates fewer by-products of oxidation, less "exhaust", so to speak. I have spoken about the low-carb, high-fat diet at numerous medical meetings regarding the treatment of obesity, diabetes, metabolic syndrome, polycystic ovary syndrome, and even the "anti-aging" conferences because there are early indications taking sugar and starches out of the diet might slow down the aging process.

The Duke Lifestyle Medicine Clinic was started in 2007 as a natural extension of the research that had been done at Duke University, and then more extensive research happening around the world. My interest in LCHF started as a doctor in a clinic—two of my patients used the Atkins Diet to lose weight, and I thought to myself how easy it would be to use this approach. But, like most physicians, I was skeptical and concerned about the fat in the diet. However if it was indeed safe, I knew that this could be an important tool to treat obesity.

Even today, the most common concern that people express about the low carbohydrate lifestyle is what will happen to their blood cholesterol level by eating all that fat. A whole generation of doctors, dietitians, and the general public were taught that eating fat and cholesterol would raise the bad blood cholesterol and cause heart disease. This was called the "diet-heart hypothesis" and was the theory that spawned the low-fat diet fad. I was privileged to be a part of the recent studies about the LCHF diet. The prediction that LCHF diets would worsen the blood lipid profile didn't come true when they were actually studied. Rather, it revealed that the LCHF diet reduced health risks by lowering the blood triglyceride and raising the good HDL cholesterol. Eating fat raises your good cholesterol!

Today, at the Duke Lifestyle Medicine Clinic, we use the LCHF diet as a therapeutic protocol to reverse most of the chronic medical conditions that are seen today. But LCHF is also a healthy diet that prevents these same chronic medical conditions. My job is to teach LCHF clearly, to taper people off medications as the medical conditions improve, and finally to make sure that people like the foods that they are eating so that they can sustain this way of eating. Because the hunger goes away after a few days of eating LCHF, most people eat less than before, and lose weight if they have excessive fat stores (obesity). The most common reason people come to see me is to lose weight. But LCHF is also excellent as a treatment for diabetes, high blood pressure, gastroesophageal reflux disorder, high blood triglycerides, low blood HDL cholesterol, polycystic ovarian syndrome, irritable bowel disease—I am continually learning about problems that can be improved by LCHF. Often the improvements that we see are "unbelievable"—meaning that other doctors and experts don't believe it. Weight loss of 200 pounds, lowering of blood triglycerides by 900 mg/dl, increasing the good HDL cholesterol of 50 mg/dL—doctors often are in disbelief, and because the studies haven't been published, the researchers say it doesn't exist. However, these are the clinical outcomes that we observe.

As of 2014, the mainstream view is changing the focus from "fat is bad" to "sugar is bad." If you've done any reading about low carbohydrate lifestyles, then you will also know that starches are digested into sugar quite efficiently—so limiting starches is just as important as limiting sugars. Rest assured that your body can rely on fat as a fuel and make all of the daily needs of sugar by itself from the fat and protein that you eat.

Let the LCHF feast begin!

Eric C. Westman, M.D., M.H.S.

Why Low Carb/High Fat?

Low Carb/High Fat. Wow! How did we get here? After all those rice cakes and bran cereals, all that fat-free milk, it turns out that fats—albeit the right fats—are far better for us than those "healthy whole grains." After a few decades of low-carb being called a "high protein diet," we're learning that a bit less protein and a bit more fat not only won't make us fat, but that it actually can also make us slimmer and improve our health in the bargain.

It happened to me. Back in 2010, I discovered that, despite my HbA1c (the measure of average blood sugar over the previous three months) being completely normal, my fasting blood glucose was running just a little high, in the pre-diabetic range.

"What's fasting blood sugar?" I hear you cry. It's blood sugar tested upon arising, when you have, presumably, been fasting for 8 or more hours. This is obviously significantly different from what's called post-prandial blood sugar —blood sugar tested after eating, when you expect blood sugar to be elevated at least a little. The American Diabetes Association considers 2-hour post-prandial blood sugar (taken 2 hours after a meal) of 180 or above to indicate diabetes. Personally, I try not to go above 120 on the advice of Dr. William Davis, cardiologist and author of *Wheat Belly*. Fasting blood sugar should be lower, of course. Between 70 and 100 is considered normal, 100 to 120 is pre-diabetic, and fasting blood sugar over 120 is a marker of diabetes. My post-prandial blood sugar was invariably golden, but my fasting blood sugar was generally between 105 and 110; I even saw it at 119 one day.

"I eat 20 to 30 grams of carbohydrate per day," I told the doctor. "Where the heck is the sugar coming from?" He replied that my liver was making it from protein via gluconeogenesis. You may have heard that carbohydrates are not essential because your liver can make glucose. It turns out that my liver is really good at it.

I hasten to repeat that overall my blood sugar was great, as demonstrated by my HbA1c. It was just the fasting blood glucose. And it was driving me crazy; I know that excess sugar is destructive and that the damage is often permanent. So I went on Metformin, but my morning sugar still ran in the pre-diabetic range. We added Victoza, too. Still, the stupid fasting blood glucose was just over normal.

Flash forward about 6 months. I wanted to knock off a quick 5 to 10 pounds before a television shoot. Yeah, I'm a whole lot thinner than I used to be, but the television camera strikes fear into the hearts of many people more beautiful than me. I decided to try the Fat Fast, as outlined by Dr. Robert Atkins in *Dr. Atkins' New Diet Revolution.* I'd known about the Fat Fast for years and had read the research that led Dr. Atkins to develop it.

So for a week or so I aimed for 1000 calories per day, 90 percent of them from fat. I lost weight like a charm, about a pound a day. I felt fine, clear-headed and energetic and even had a great weight-lifting workout one day.

But far more exciting, my fasting blood sugar was normal. Normal-normal-normal.

After the television shoot, I continued eating a higher percentage of fat. I dropped my daily protein intake from an average of 120 grams to 60 to 90 grams, adding butter, cream, avocados, nuts, and oils to make up the missing calories. Instead of a whole rib-eye steak, I'd have half a steak with butter melted over it—such deprivation.

And my morning sugar stayed normal. Indeed, it started to run a little low. I dropped the Victoza, then the Metformin. My fasting sugar hung in the 85 to 95 range. It continues to do so till this day. I had a full blood panel done recently, and my new doctor was a little nonplussed by the results: rock-bottom triglycerides, sky-high HDL, all measures of liver and kidney health perfect, low CRP (the measure of inflammation), and my HbA1c as low as they measure it. She actually said, "This blood work is something to be proud of." She was curious but accepting when I told her I'd done it by melting butter over steaks.

I think I can confidently state that a low-carb, high-fat diet is good for me.

I'm not the only one. Superstar low-carb blogger and podcaster Jimmy Moore did a yearlong self-experiment with nutritional ketosis, testing his blood rather than his urine (this is far more accurate) and discovered that he needed to eat a lot more fat to be in deep ketosis. When he jacked up his fat intake and got his blood ketones where he wanted them, he shed 70 pounds he'd been struggling with. He looks amazing.

Not Just Weight Loss

But the implications are far greater. Low-carb/high-fat, strongly ketogenic diets, long used for seizure control, are showing promise for treating all sorts of health problems.

> A study published in 2011 in the scientific journal *PLOS One* looked at the effects of a ketogenic diet on diabetic nephropathy—the most common cause of kidney failure—in diabetic mice. What was the result? Two months on a ketogenic diet actually reversed kidney damage. This had hitherto been virtually unheard of.

> In August 2013, *The Clinical Journal of the American Society of Nephrology* published the results of a small human trial, again showing an improvement in kidney function in type 2 diabetics with nephropathy after 12 weeks on a ketogenic diet. I find this not only wonderful but also happily ironic considering how many times I've been told my diet will damage my kidneys.

> In 2012, in the journal *Nutrition*, Drs. Richard D. Feinman and Eugene Fine published groundbreaking work regarding the effectiveness of such diets in inhibiting cancer growth by reducing insulin signaling.

> In 2006, the journal *Behavioral Pharmacology* published an article about the benefits of a ketogenic diet for a broad range of neurological illnesses. Ketogenic diets have long been used to treat epilepsy, but they are now showing promise for treating Parkinson's disease and Alzheimer's as well. Having watched my mother succumb to dementia, this is, for me, the most thrilling possibility.

> The same article also states that ketogenic diets are being explored for limiting inflammation in general. Since inflammation now appears to be the root of a great deal of illness, from heart disease to cancer, this is no small thing.

> In 2005, *Nutrition & Metabolism* published an article regarding a pilot study of a ketogenic diet for treatment of polycystic ovarian syndrome (PCOS). The study found that the diet not only caused "significant" weight loss but also improved hormone balance and lowered fasting insulin.

The Hardest Part

While doing the Fat Fast, I found that the hardest part wasn't eating just 1,000 or so calories per day; due to ketones suppressing appetite, that was easier than I expected. No, the hard part was getting 90 percent of my calories from fat. Unless you like olive oil shooters, it takes some doing. Most days I would hit around the 85 percent mark, which worked just fine. Since completing the Fat Fast, I don't restrict calories most of the time, and I aim for 75 percent or more of my calories from fat.

Even this is harder than it sounds. So often fat comes paired with carbohydrates: bread with garlic butter, French fries, fettuccine Alfredo. These foods may be high in fat, but they're even higher in carbohydrate, and that carbohydrate can trigger your body to store the calories, including the fat calories, as fat. This is an important point, so let me be very clear: Adding lots of extra fat to your diet without simultaneously slashing carbs will make you gain weight, not lose it.

So what are the secrets of jacking up the fat in your diet without adding carbs? And how do you do it in a sustainable, healthful way? That's what this book is all about.

We're Talking Percentage of Calories, Not Volume or Weight

It's important to understand that we're talking percentage of total calories, rather than percentage by weight or volume. For example: 4 ounces (115 g) of green beans will have 31 calo-ries, with 7 grams of carbohydrate, 2 grams of protein, and only a trace of fat. This translates to those beans getting 78 percent of their calories from carbohydrate and only 3 percent from fat.

But because fats are very calorically dense, adding only ½ ounce (15 g) of butter and ½ ounce (15 g) of slivered almonds will create a dish with 216 calories, 75 percent of them from fat. Bring on the green beans almondine!

Please note that in this example, those green beans actually have 3 grams of fiber, a carbohydrate that most of us subtract from our total carbs. Because my MasterCook software doesn't take this into account, the ratios in this book will not be calculated on net or usable carbs, but on total carbs. Why? Because I don't want to do that much math, that's why. However, if you'd like to do it yourself, here's how:

Assume that carbohydrate and protein have 4 calories per gram and fats have 9 calories per gram. This is only loosely true, but for our purposes it is near enough. So, we have 216 calories total, but we want to subtract the 3 grams of fiber. $3 \times 4 = 12$, so we subtract 12 calories, for a total of 204. Our green beans almondine contain 19 grams of fat. $19 \times 9 = 171$. To figure out what percentage of the adjusted calorie count that constitutes, divide 171 by 204. According to my trusty calculator, that gives us 84 percent of calories from fat. All of the recipes in this book list the carb, fiber, and fat grams, so if you want to make these calculations, you certainly may. Me, I just figure my fat percentage is a little higher than the software tells me, and I don't sweat it.

A Gentle Warning

We tend to think of only fat, protein, and carbohydrate as contributing calories, but there is one other substance that contains considerable calories: alcohol. At 7 calories per gram, alcohol is more calorically dense than anything but fats. If you're drinking, you skew your ratios; it's hard to get your fat percentage up to 75 percent. (We won't even talk about the carbohydrates that many alcoholic beverages bring along.) I like wine as much as the next girl, but alcohol is a luxury on a weight-loss diet, no matter how you look at it.

Ways to Increase Fat Intake

It's not essential that every dish be over 75 percent fat. You can combine dishes to get the percentages you're looking for. For instance, a piece of roasted chicken gets about 55 percent of its calories from fat. But pair it with a green salad with plenty of olive oil and the percentage for your meal can easily go up to 75 percent.

Make use of naturally high-fat foods: Nuts, bacon, avocados, olives, and fatty cheeses all add flavor and texture to your meals along with the fat you seek. You'll find them used in abundance in these recipes. You can use heavy cream or full-fat coconut milk in your coffee, too.

Fat is a very concentrated source of nutrients:

2 tablespoons (28 g) of butter or (28 ml) oil will have 200 calories or more. Fat will quell your hunger, but most of us want to eat more than that. Yet you don't want to blow past either your carb limit or your protein requirement. So, how do you get a full plate of food? Think water and fiber. Both water and fiber contribute no calories, no carbs, no protein, no nuthin', to your meal, yet they can expand your portions deliciously to satisfying proportions.

Low-carb vegetables are largely made up of water and fiber, and they make a great fat-delivery system: for example, salads with plenty of olive oil or mayonnaise, vegetables with butter, and celery with pâté or blue cheese dip. You get the picture—serve your vegetables with fat. Interestingly, this will greatly enhance your body's absorption of fat-soluble vitamins and antioxidants.

Think about it: 2 tablespoons (28 g) of mayonnaise has 200 calories, 99 percent of them from fat. But while those 2 tablespoons (28 g) of mayo will keep you full and energetic for quite a while, they're barely more than a mouthful. Add a cup (70 g) of shredded cabbage, and suddenly you have a big ol' portion of coleslaw, while adding only 15 calories and 4 grams carbohydrate, 2 of 'em being fiber, resulting in just 2 grams of usable carb.

Likewise, broths are mostly water. (Homemade bone broth is mostly water, gelatin, calcium, and sheer magic.) A half a cup (120 ml) of coconut milk has 222 calories, 91 percent of them from fat, with just 3 grams of carb. But who drinks ½ cup (120 ml) of coconut milk and feels like she's had a meal? Combine that coconut milk with 1 cup (235 ml) of chicken broth, plus curry powder and a touch of garlic, and you've got a fabulous, warming soup.

Use sauces and dips to your advantage; you'll find plenty of them in this book. Sirloin steak gets 63 percent of its calories from fat. Add a couple of tablespoons (28 g) of blue cheese butter, and that goes up to 74 percent. Two cups (110 g) of lettuce have 20 calories, only 12 percent of them from fat. Add 2 tablespoons (28 ml) vinaigrette dressing and that jumps to 160 calories, 85 percent of them from fat.

Choose fatty cuts of meat—pork shoulder or spareribs, chicken and turkey dark meat with the skin on, rib-eye steak, chuck, and brisket, 70/30 ground beef instead of the pricey 90/10 stuff, and of course, everybody's favorite, bacon. If you're choosing a lower-fat protein—fish, chicken breast, or the like—again, use a fatty sauce and add a salad or vegetable with a fatty dressing on the side.

Your meals will be very nutrient dense and high in calories. This is okay; if you pay attention to your hunger, you will very quickly learn to eat to satiety, rather than eating just because the food is there. I have long since reached the point where I eat two good-size meals per day, with a snack if I'm feeling peckish in between. If you're used to the constant, driving hunger of a low-fat diet based on grains, this will seem incredible,

even impossible. Don't force it. Just shift your macronutrient balance and pay attention to your hunger.

How High in Fat Are These Recipes?

I've mostly kept them in the range of 70 percent of calories from fat or higher, but there are some exceptions. Why? Sometimes, as with crackers, I made an exception because I felt the recipes filled an important culinary niche, and they would probably be eaten with something fatty anyway. Sometimes it was because, hey, it's 68 percent, and geez, I think it's a good recipe.

For Fat Fasters

Because these recipes dip as low as the high 60-something percent range in fat content, not all of them are appropriate for fat fasting. For those of you who are fat fasting, I have highlighted fat percentages over 80 percent so that you can easily pick out the suitable recipes. It's up to you to stick to 200-calorie portions.

On Taking Control

Celebrity chef Emeril Lagasse likes to say, regarding various seasonings, "You want more? Put in more. You want a little less? Use less.

Hey, we're just cooking, it's not rocket science." These are words to live by.

I love cilantro; it tastes like the very essence of fresh and green to me. But if you're one of those people who thinks cilantro tastes like soap, leave it out. I've been known to get up in the morning and eat a jalapeño and Monterey Jack omelet with salsa and habanero hot sauce because I love breathing fire. You don't? Cut back on the hot sauce. You think I'm a big wussy? Add more.

As my professional idol Peg Bracken said, it's all a matter of deciding who's in charge here, you or the food.

Regarding Microwave Ovens

I use my microwave all the time, not just for reheating leftovers, but also for cooking, especially for steaming vegetables. I know of no simpler nor more satisfactory method, and my Tupperware microwave steamer is out of the cabinet more often than in it. Furthermore, I have seen some fairly convincing arguments stating that microwave steaming of vegetables retains more nutrients than most other cooking methods.

I also often cook bacon in the microwave; I haunted the local thrift store until I found a circular microwave bacon tray that would go around on my microwave's turntable.

However, I suspect that at least some of you will be appalled that I would even consider using a microwave. There is a faction that considers them, and all food cooked in them, to be horribly dangerous. I'm not going to argue the point here. Just take it as a given that anything I direct to cook in the microwave, you are welcome to cook on your stovetop.

Pantry Essentials

Most of the ingredients in this book will be familiar to you, especially if you've been eating a low-carb diet for a while. But there are a few that could use a little explanation—some are new to the market in the past few years, and some are traditional ingredients that have been vilified since the 1970s, when the whole anti-saturated-fat-and-cholesterol nonsense began. Here's a briefing.

Which Fats Should I Use?

When you're deliberately eating a high-fat diet, it is a good idea to pay attention to the quality of those fats. Unfortunately, officialdom has misinformed us about "healthy fats" for a good 30 years now. We were told to drastically limit "artery-clogging saturated fats" and substitute unsaturated vegetable oils. This led to the current disastrous imbalance of unsaturated fatty acids in the American diet; the optimal 1:1 ratio of omega-3 and omega-6 fatty acids has been skewed to an average of 15:1. The result is a harvest of all kinds of inflammatory illnesses, including cardiovascular disease, cancer, and autoimmune illnesses.

The demonizing of traditional animal fats was to a great degree driven by the burgeoning vegetable oil industry. Are you old enough to remember ads crowing about how polyunsaturated this or that vegetable oil was? Have you noticed that those ads have passed quietly from our midst? Margarine ads have been radically reduced, as well. You know why?

Because it turns out that swapping in highly processed vegetable oils for traditional animal fats like butter, lard, tallow, and chicken fat is terrible for you, increasing the risk of everything from heart disease to cancer. Oops.

I trust you know, too, that substituting trans fat–rich hydrogenated vegetable shortening for naturally saturated fats has turned out to be a disaster.

In this book, we return to traditional fats. Following is the rundown on what I have mostly used.

Butter: I don't need to tell you that butter tastes wonderful, but perhaps you need to be told that it is healthful as well. We'll start with the fact that butter is a good source of vitamin A—true, preformed vitamin A rather than the "provitamin A" you get from plant sources. It's also a source of vitamin E, a powerful antioxidant, and vitamin K, essential for calcium absorption, creating strong bones and teeth. This is especially true if the butter is from grass-fed cows. Butter is also a source of selenium and iodine, the main constituents of thyroid hormone.

What about saturated fat? Butter is rich in saturated fats, it's true—about 60 percent of the fatty acids in butter are saturated. Interestingly, quite a lot of that is in the form of lauric acid. More than any other fat tested, lauric acid raises HDL cholesterol, which is thought to lower heart disease risk. There is some feeling that lauric acid has other benefits, ranging from antimicrobial and antifungal activity to stimulating the thyroid gland, thus raising metabolism.

Then there's conjugated linoleic acid (CLA), a naturally occurring trans fat that is not only harmless, but actually beneficial. When CLA was first identified in the 1980s, it was shown to help prevent and even treat cancer; there were gleeful headlines about how Velveeta was a cancer cure. Exaggerated, of course, but the benefits of CLA are real.

Further testing of CLA has repeatedly demonstrated a positive effect on body composition, reducing fat, especially belly fat, and increasing muscle mass.

Grass-fed raw butter is higher in nutrients than the standard grocery store stuff and worth the extra money. Raw dairy products are banned in many states, but grass-fed butter is pretty widely available. I know people who buy the popular Kerrygold grass-fed butter a dozen bars at a time. Living, as I do, in the Midwest, there are many local small farms producing butter of excellent quality. Check health food stores and farmers' markets or look online for local small dairies.

Ghee: Also called clarified butter, ghee is butter that has had all the milk solids removed, leaving only the fats. This makes ghee less likely to spoil than butter (useful in warm climates like India) and less likely to burn. Because the milk solids have been removed, ghee is well tolerated by many people who are lactose intolerant; I know many people who avoid dairy products except for ghee.

Ghee is available in jars in stores that carry a selection of Indian foods and ingredients. Once opened, it should be refrigerated. You can make your own ghee quite easily: Melt butter over very low heat. Let the light-colored solids sink to the bottom, pour off the liquid butterfat into a container, and discard the solids.

Like butter, ghee is most nutritious if it comes from grass-fed cows.

Lard: Yes, lard. Until Americans were sold a bill of goods about vegetable oils and hydrogenated shortening, lard was the most-used fat in the American diet, not only for frying and sautéing, but also as shortening in baked goods. My grandma used it in piecrust. It is lard that Crisco and other hydrogenated shortenings supplanted in American cooking. Lard was also spread on bread, just like butter, and still is in much of the world.

Yet lard has been so defamed that it has become symbolic of "artery-clogging saturated fat," though ironically it has slightly more unsaturated than saturated fat—about 57 percent. Most of that unsaturated fat in lard is in the form of monounsaturates, the same sort of fat that is considered healthful when found in olive oil. Unfortunately, most of the lard in grocery stores cannot be considered a good fat. Not only does it come from animals raised on the cheapest, nastiest feed, but much of it is also hydrogenated, specifically because lard is unsaturated enough to be soft at room temperature. So don't buy cheap grocery store lard that's sitting on the shelf next to the vegetable shortening.

Seek out a local small farm that produces pasture-raised pork and buy a bucket of unprocessed lard. This is glorious stuff, bland yet rich, wonderful for all kinds of sautéing, basting, and even baking. It's worth the money: At this writing, I pay about $15 for a 4-pound (1.8 kg) bucket of lard from locally raised pastured pigs.

Because lard is rich in monounsaturates, it will go rancid eventually. Scoop out enough for a week or so, put it in a clean jar, and freeze the rest.

Bonus: Since pigs, like us, create vitamin D in their skin when exposed to sunlight, that vitamin D is stored in their fat. This means that lard from pasture-raised pigs is one of the few naturally rich food sources of vitamin D. (The vitamin D in milk is the result of supplementation.)

Bacon Grease: Lard with a salty, smoky, amazing flavor, bacon grease is pure culinary gold. If you shell out the money for good, small-farm bacon from pastured hogs, and then throw out the grease, I will personally come to your house and dope-slap you. Around here, we keep the stuff from cheap grocery store bacon, too. I pour it into an old salsa jar, keep it by the stove, and use it for all sorts of things, from frying eggs to roasting vegetables. I'd refrigerate it, but I use it up too fast for it to go bad.

Olive Oil: It's hard to get a handle on olive oil. The common wisdom is that it's the healthiest possible fat, but the paleo faction disputes that, especially if used for cooking rather than in uncooked applications like salad dressings. I'm of the opinion that olive oil has been around long enough to be considered pretty safe, and the flavor is essential to Mediterranean and Middle Eastern cuisines, of which I am seriously fond. I use it for salad dressings and in cooking where the flavor is essential to the dish.

Coconut Oil: Coconut oil is a favorite of the low-carb, high-fat set and with good reason. Coconut oil is very healthful stuff. It is high in lauric acid, with all its benefits. It raises your HDL cholesterol levels (the good stuff), increases immunity, improves insulin sensitivity, and stimulates the thyroid gland. Most of the saturated fat in coconut oil is in the form of medium-chain triglycerides (MCT), a fat that can be used directly by the muscles for fuel—it's true energy food. MCT is also highly ketogenic.

Coconut oil is very saturated, far more so than lard, beef fat, or butter, and it turns out that this is a good thing. Saturated fats barely oxidize, you see, eliminating the risk of rancid fats. Even at room temperature, coconut oil will keep for as long as a year. Coconut oil is solid below 76°F (24°C), making it inappropriate for salad dressings. It's great for all sorts of cooking applications, though. It's a terrific substitute for hydrogenated shortenings (Crisco and the like) in baking.

I find two kinds of coconut oil in my local stores: Some is labeled extra-virgin coconut

oil, while the rest is simply labeled coconut oil. Extra-virgin is nutritionally superior, but it has a mild but distinct coconut fragrance and flavor. Depending on the recipe and your tastes, this may or may not work for you. The stuff labeled coconut oil has been refined and is bland. While it is not as nutritionally pristine as the extra-virgin stuff, I still consider plain old coconut oil to be a healthy fat and keep it on hand.

I have used coconut oil extensively in this book because it's convenient and healthful. However, you can feel free to substitute another bland fat like lard or chicken fat for sautéing. Who am I to judge?

In my area, extra-virgin coconut oil is found in health food stores, while the refined stuff is found in the international aisle (it's a staple of Indian cooking) of our local international/health food grocery store, Sahara Mart. (Unpaid plug and shout-out—I love Sahara Mart.) My local Kroger also carries refined coconut oil with the other oils, so its availability is increasing in the big supermarket chains.

Medium-Chain Triglyceride Oil: Derived from coconut oil, MCT oil has been popular with athletes for a while because it can be burned directly by the muscles, offering a quick burst of energy without the crash that sugar would bring. It is also used for people who need concentrated nutrition; it can be particularly useful in cancer patients, for instance. Because MCT oil is highly ketogenic, it is also a great choice for anyone who wishes to keep a high blood ketone level; to treat epilepsy, Alzheimer's, or cancer; or just to maintain high energy and suppress hunger.

Because it is concentrated, MCT oil is even more ketogenic than coconut oil. Unlike coconut oil, MCT oil is liquid at room temperature, making it useful for salad dressings and the like. It is quite bland, so if you're not crazy about the strong flavor of olive oil in mayonnaise, MCT oil is a good choice.

A word to the wise: I paid about $20 for three 1-quart (950 ml) bottles of MCT oils during a good sale at a mail-order supplement house, and I regularly see it going for $10 per quart (950 ml) online. In the meanwhile, my pharmacy has a bottle of the stuff behind the counter with a price tag of $91. So, shop around.

Sunflower Oil: I occasionally use Spectrum brand organic, high-temperature sunflower oil when I want a bland liquid oil. Most vegetable oils are high in polyunsaturates, meaning they are pro-inflammatory, but the Spectrum sunflower is mostly monounsaturated, with only a very little polyunsaturated fat. Spectrum is a health food store brand, but my local large grocery stores carry it as well.

Other Fats to Consider

I haven't used them in these recipes, but other traditional fats include the following:

Chicken Fat: Also known as schmaltz, rendered chicken fat is a staple of Jewish cuisine. Whether you can find it in local stores may depend upon whether you live where there is a substantial Jewish population. Good specialty butchers should have this, too. Properly rendered, chicken fat is a bland, neutral fat that can be used in a wide variety of foods—my mother claimed her mother used it as shortening in brownies!

Again, the quality of the chicken fat will depend on how the chicken was raised. No hormones, antibiotics, or soy feed will make for more healthful schmaltz.

Duck Fat: If you roast a duck, do not, I say *do not* throw away the fat. Use it for sautéing and roasting vegetables. It's amazing. And ducks have a lot of fat!

Tallow: Remember how good McDonald's fries were when you were a kid? You know why? They were fried in tallow, also known as beef fat. In the 1980s, the OMG-Saturated-Fat-Is-Eeeevul Squad bullied them into switching to hydrogenated vegetable oil, which not only made the fries less tasty, but filled them with trans fats, too. Especially if you can get fat from grass-fed beef, it's an excellent cooking fat. Indeed, you should make it a rule never to discard fat from properly raised meat.

Lemon-Flavored Cod Liver Oil: Look for the Carlson brand. I haven't tried it yet, though I've been taking cod liver oil capsules for years, but I've had enough people I trust tell me it tastes really good—good enough to use on salads or drizzle over chicken or fish—that I'm going to get some. It's not for cooking with!

On the Interchangeability of Fats

If I call for coconut oil for sautéing, and you want to use lard, or chicken fat, or tallow, go ahead, okay? I won't care, and your recipe will come out fine.

Regarding Vegetable Oils

There are other vegetable oils I'd be willing to use—macadamia nut oil, for one, or walnut oil if a recipe specified it. Or avocado oil. Still, in general, I prefer the fats I've just listed; most vegetable oils in quantity have to be considered experimental in the human diet.

Here's my rough rule: If I can figure out how they got the oil out of the source, I'm probably willing to use it, at least in limited quantity. If you rub a piece of coconut or a walnut meat or an avocado on a piece of paper, you'll get a grease spot. Heck, you can practically squeeze the oil out of olives right there in your kitchen.

Can you figure out how you'd get oil out of a soybean or an ear of corn? I've never found those things to be oily, have you? I'm not even sure what a safflower is. As for "canola," it's a hybrid of a plant that has the unfortunate name *rape*. Rapeseed oil has historically been used as varnish but had been considered too toxic for human consumption because of a constituent called erucic acid. It was also bitter and unpleasant tasting. Canola is the trade name

of a low–erucic acid hybrid of rapeseed initially bred for use in animal feed and then eventually marketed for human consumption. I've heard some dire stories about canola, but like so much Weblore they strike me as questionable. What is not in question is that canola oil is novel in the human diet, and it has been highly processed. I don't use it.

The most important thing is to stay away from excessive polyunsaturated oils. They are highly inflammatory.

Other Ingredients

Now that we've slid past the fats, let's talk about a few other ingredients that may need clarification. These are just things I've received questions about over the years or that have changed in the course of my career. Perhaps the most complex, and often the most controversial, is sweeteners, so let's tackle them first.

Sweeteners

Here's my confession: I still like Splenda. I remain unconvinced that, in the modest quantities in which I historically have used it, sucralose is hideously dangerous. I think it tastes good, and I find it easy to use. However, I do not write recipes for me, I write them for you. So many of you have let me know that you no longer use sucralose that I don't generally use it for developing recipes for publication anymore.

So what am I using?

LIQUID STEVIA

While I found the old-school highly concentrated powdered stevia difficult to use, the liquid stevia extracts in dropper bottles are far easier and taste far better. Furthermore, they come in a broad array of flavors. The ones I keep on hand and have used in this book are as follows:

> **Plain:** That is, it's just sweet. I've been using NuNaturals brand plain liquid stevia. This is great when you want a touch of sweetness in a recipe, without any other flavor overtones.

> **English Toffee:** I use this constantly. Why? Because the flavor bears a similarity to brown sugar.

> **Vanilla:** The uses for a sweetener with a vanilla flavor added should be obvious! I do often add vanilla extract, as well. I also often combine vanilla stevia with English toffee or with…

> **Chocolate:** Again, the uses here are obvious, from hot cocoa to cookies.

> **Lemon Drop:** This is good not only in lemon-flavored recipes, but also in all sorts of recipes with a fruit flavor.

I can buy all of these flavors and more at Sahara Mart, my beloved local health/international/gourmet grocery. If your health food store doesn't carry these, they can very likely order them for you; most health food stores are awesome about special orders. Ask them about NOW and SweetLeaf brands.

If you're not blessed with a great local health food store, you can order these items from Amazon.com, like everything else on the planet. I checked Netrition.com and found only the plain stevia extracts, but that may change; it's worth looking again.

It's helpful to have an idea of how many drops of a given brand of stevia are roughly equal to 1 teaspoon of sugar in sweetness. These recipes assume liquid stevia of a sweetness so that 6 drops = 1 teaspoon of sugar. I start with ¼ teaspoon of stevia to replace ¼ cup (50 g) sugar and ½ teaspoon stevia to replace ½ cup (100 g) sugar. If your liquid stevia is considerably more or less sweet than this, you will need to adjust quantities. Look at the manufacturer's Web site for equivalencies.

Again, this applies only to the liquid extracts! If you put that much of the concentrated white stevia powder in a recipe, it is likely to be inedible.

EZ Sweetz makes a good liquid stevia, but it is stronger than what I've been using: 2 drops = 1 teaspoon sugar. They also make a mixed stevia-monkfruit extract of about the same concentration.

If you prefer, you can use liquid sucralose or monkfruit extract in place of liquid stevia. You will, however, need to know the conversion factor. For instance, with EZ Sweetz liquid sucralose, only 1 drop is required to equal 1 teaspoon of sugar or 12 drops to equal ¼ cup (50 g).

ERYTHRITOL

Of all the sugar alcohols, aka polyols, erythritol has the least blood sugar impact because it is neither digested nor absorbed, but rather simply passed through. By contrast, you absorb roughly half of maltitol, the sugar alcohol most used in commercial sugar-free sweets, so it cannot be completely discounted. Too, unlike maltitol, which is notorious for its embarrassing and even uncomfortable gastric effects, erythritol causes virtually no gut upset.

These two qualities have made erythritol a real comer in the burgeoning sugar-free sweetener market; it has been one of the sweeteners I reach for most often for a few years now.

So why hasn't erythritol supplanted maltitol in commercial sweets? It's harder to work with. Maltitol behaves remarkably like sugar in cooking; you can get all the textures of sugar—gooey caramels, silky sauces, crunchy brittles. Erythritol melts in warm mixtures, but it has a tendency to recrystallize as it cools, making final results grainy.

Most confounding, erythritol has the peculiar property of being endothermic, meaning that when it hits the moisture in your mouth, it quite literally absorbs energy, creating a cooling sensation. This works well in ice cream but can be a little disconcerting in a cookie.

There's one more hitch: Erythritol is not quite as sweet as sugar, being about 70 percent as sweet.

All of this explains why I usually combine erythritol with liquid stevia. Indeed, the industry does as well; Truvia is a combination of erythritol and stevia. (Why didn't I use Truvia in these recipes? I'm just not crazy about the flavor of the stuff; I find it bitter.)

Of the erythritol products I have used, my favorite by far is one called Swerve, a combination of erythritol and oligosaccharides, a sweet-tasting fiber. Swerve measures like sugar and because of the oligosaccharides, it browns. Swerve comes both in a granular version and a powdered confectioner's-style version. Because of the potential for graininess with erythritol, I generally prefer powdered Swerve, though I keep both versions on hand. (No, I do not get a kickback from Swerve. Not even a free bag. I just think the stuff is really good.)

The main drawback of Swerve is the price; the stuff is not cheap. Because I don't use a ton of sweeteners when I'm not working on a book, this is not a major issue for me, but it may be for you.

I buy Swerve at my health food store, but you may not find it locally. You should be able to special-order the stuff through your local health food store and you can order it through Amazon.com and also from Netrition.com.

Plain erythritol, though not cheap, is less expensive than Swerve—I pay about $12 per pound for Swerve, and I have seen erythritol as cheap as $7 per pound. Again, this is a health food store item. You can substitute plain erythritol for Swerve in most of these recipes, though they won't brown as much, and you may want to increase the stevia a little bit.

There is powdered erythritol on the market; I recommend it, because of the possibility of graininess. I have also made powdered erythritol from granular by running it through my food processor until it's powdery. Your results may depend on the quality of your food processor.

WHY NOT XYLITOL?

I've been asked why I don't use xylitol instead of erythritol. Some people prefer xylitol, and it does have the big advantage of actually remineralizing tooth enamel. However, xylitol is partially absorbed in the gut, rather than being passed through, and it has the much-dreaded polyol laxative effect. It also has the same cooling effect as erythritol, so no advantage there.

However, the main reason I don't use xylitol is that it is profoundly toxic to dogs, and I have three. If one of them stole a cookie and died, I would never forgive myself. If you do use xylitol, be very careful to keep it away from your canine pals.

SUGAR-FREE IMITATION HONEY

This is just what it sounds like: a syrup of either maltitol or xylitol, depending on the brand, that is flavored like honey and behaves like honey in cooking. I've only used this in a few recipes in this book, but they're awfully good recipes.

I use HoneyTree brand, which is maltitol based. My grocery store carries this with the diabetic products. I understand some Walmart stores carry

it as well. Netrition.com carries Nature's Hollow brand, which is made of xylitol, if you prefer.

And do I need to say it again? Amazon.com carries everything. I swear, I could order a baby elephant from Amazon if I tried.

Xanthan, Guar, Glucomannan

What the heck are these? They're finely milled soluble fibers, and they're hugely useful in low-carb cuisine. These are what you use in place of flour, cornstarch, or arrowroot for thickening sauces or soups. What do they taste like? Nothing at all—they couldn't be blander if they tried. They are far more powerful thickeners than flour or the others, however, so do not try a one-for-one substitution. The results could be used to surface roads. Instead, fill an old salt or spice shaker with whichever you have on hand—I marginally prefer xanthan—and keep it by the stove. When you have a sauce or soup you need to thicken, start whisking first and then *lightly* sprinkle the thickener over the surface as you whisk. Go slowly; it's easy to put in more and impossible to remove too much. Keep in mind that these continue to thicken a bit on standing, so quit when your dish is a little less thick than you want it to be.

Unlike starchy thickeners, these do not need to cook to thicken or to get rid of a raw taste, so they can also be used in cold applications like smoothies.

These also have another use: They lend structure to baked goods based on nut meal or seed meal. In the baked goods chapter, I've used small quantities of these repeatedly to improve the texture of the finished product.

All three of these thickeners will keep pretty much forever so long as they're dry. And again, these are all health food store items, and all of them can be ordered online, too. What can't these days?

Shirataki Noodles

Most low-carb noodles are nothing I'll eat. There is one widely distributed brand, made with the same ingredients as standard pasta, that I doubt is anywhere near as low-carb as its label claims. The only noodles I eat are shirataki, and they are a staple in my kitchen.

Shirataki are traditional Japanese noodles made from the fiber glucomannan, derived from *konjac* or *konyaku*, a root vegetable. (This is often translated as "yam," but *konjac* is a completely different plant.) Being made almost entirely of fiber, shirataki are very low in both carbohydrate and calories.

Shirataki come in two basic varieties: traditional and tofu. Traditional shirataki are made entirely of glucomannan fiber. They're translucent and kind of gelatinous, really quite different from the wheat-based noodles we grew up on. I only like traditional shirataki in Asian recipes —sesame noodles, Asian soups, and the like. Tofu shirataki, as the name suggests, have a

little bit of tofu added to the glucomannan. This makes them white and gives them a more tender texture than traditional shirataki. They're not identical to "regular" pasta, but they're closer, and I like them in all sorts of things, from fettuccine Alfredo to tuna casserole. Both traditional and tofu shirataki come in a variety of widths and shapes.

Unlike the pasta you're used to, shirataki come pre-hydrated in a pouch of liquid. To use them, snip open the pouch and dump them into a strainer in the sink. You'll notice that the liquid smells fishy. Do not panic. Rinse your noodles well and put them in a microwaveable bowl. Nuke them on High for 2 minutes and drain them again. Nuke them for *another* 2 minutes and drain them one more time. This renders them quite bland and also cooks out extra liquid that would otherwise dilute any sauce you put on them.

Long noodles are considered good luck in Japan, but I find shirataki a bit too long. I snip across them a few times with my kitchen shears. All of this microwaving and draining and snipping takes less time than boiling water for standard pasta.

I find shirataki especially useful when I want to increase my fat percentage for the day. Because the shirataki themselves have almost no carbs or calories, they don't "dilute" the fat you add to them. A bowl of shirataki with a fatty sauce, or just with butter and Parmesan, makes a satisfying meal.

I can get shirataki at both my local health food stores and Asian markets. If you can't find them locally, you can order them online, but be aware: They do not tolerate freezing; they disintegrate into mush. This means you may not want to order them in the dead of winter. On the other hand, they keep for months in the fridge, so if you decide you like them, go ahead and stock up.

Coconut

I use a lot of coconut in this book; it's nutritious and highly versatile. Most of it is finely shredded coconut. One or two recipes call for flaked coconut, which is coarser. Both of these are unsweetened! Do not use the "angel flake" coconut in the baking aisle at the grocery store! It is sweetened.

It's worth shopping around for your coconut. Around here, one of the health food stores carries shredded coconut only in 12-ounce (340 g) packets for something like $5. The other one sells coconut in the bulk section, where I can scoop it out of a bin for a big $3 per pound.

Coconut keeps well—because the fat in it is so saturated, it doesn't go rancid—but it does lose water. You may find your batter or dough a little dry. Buying only as much as you'll use up in a month or so, and buying from a store with a brisk turnover, should take care of that.

Coconut Milk

Full of MCT-rich coconut oil, coconut milk is a wildly versatile ingredient, useful in everything from coffee drinks to curries. It is especially useful for those of you who are avoiding dairy. While coconut milk has its own flavor, it gives a similar creamy texture to all kinds of recipes. It also can be cultured to create cocoyo—a yogurt substitute—and coconut sour cream; see instructions page 187.

While there is now pourable coconut milk in cartons widely available, I have used only the thick canned coconut milk in these recipes. This should be available in the international aisle of your large grocery store with the Thai or Indian ingredients, at health food stores, and at Asian markets. I was pleased to find recently that Kroger, the nation's biggest grocery chain, now carries a house brand of coconut milk.

I find coconut milk in both 14-fluid ounce (410 ml) and 13.5-fluid ounce (350 ml) cans. Trust me, half an ounce of coconut milk one way or the other is not going to spoil your dish. Don't sweat it. Do I need to tell you to buy full-fat coconut milk, not light?

Coconut Flour

I've used coconut flour in just a few recipes; this is milled from what's left after the oil is pressed out of coconut. It is quite low in carbs and very high in fiber. Bob's Red Mill brand is widely distributed.

I've been asked why I don't use coconut flour more in my baked goods. Honestly, it's because I'm not crazy about the results, and the stuff has a steep learning curve. I find almond meal, vanilla whey, and some other flour substitutes more agreeable. But if you'd like to pursue coconut flour further, there are a few coconut flour cookbooks out there—Bruce Fife's is probably the best known.

Flaxseed Meal

This is pretty easy to get these days; all my local grocery stores have it in the baking aisle. I use Bob's Red Mill brand golden flaxseed meal; I like it, and it's easy to find.

Vanilla Whey Protein Powder

A few of these recipes call for vanilla whey protein powder. I've used several brands over the years, and I've never had one not work in a recipe. Designer Whey Protein is perhaps most widely available; GNC stores carry it. Recently, I've been using Vitacost.com's house brand because the price is right, and it works fine.

Rice Protein Powder

I've used rice protein in one or two recipes. Nutribiotic makes this, and it's available through health food stores and, of course, online. There are flavored versions, but you're looking for the plain version for these recipes. The whole point is to have a bland low-carb flour substitute. Generally, both the rice protein powder and the vanilla whey powder are sold in canisters that hold 1 pound (455 g) or more. So long as you keep them lidded and in a dry place, they should keep for a long, long time. I think my jar of rice protein is at least 3 years old, and my recipes come out well.

Bouillon Concentrate

I use bouillon concentrate as a seasoning all the time. You can use bouillon granules or liquid, but my preferred form is Better Than Bouillon paste: It actually contains some of the protein source listed on the label and is gluten-free, and I think the flavor is superior to granules or cubes. I keep beef and chicken Better Than Bouillon pastes on hand.

If you're eating paleo, or just "clean," there's a simple substitute for bouillon concentrate: reduced stock. The easiest way I know to make this is to put good strong chicken or beef stock in your slow cooker, on Low, with the lid off, and let it cook down till it's syrupy. Store this in a lidded jar in the freezer and use just like you would bouillon concentrate—which is, after all, what it is. How salty homemade reduced stock will be will depend on the saltiness of the stock you start with.

Creole Seasoning

I've been known to make my own, but generally I use Tony Cachere's "spicier" blend. It's widely available. Use a milder version if you're not as devoted to hot food as I am.

Vege-Sal

One of my favorite seasonings, Vege-Sal is a blend of salt and powdered vegetables. It's subtle, but I think it improves many savory dishes, and you'll see that I often have specified "salt or Vege-Sal."

Vege-Sal is made by Modern Products, and the company has recently had their popular "Spike" name added to the title, so it's "Spike Vege-Sal." If your health food store doesn't have it, they can order it for you, or you can order it online. Or just use salt.

If you're going to try Vege-Sal, be aware that in addition to coming in a shaker, it's available in 10-ounce (280 g) or 20-ounce (560 g) boxes. If you decide you like it, this is considerably cheaper than buying a shaker every time you need Vege-Sal!

Be aware that Vege-Sal does contain a bit of hydrolyzed soy protein. This doesn't scare me, considering how little I'm consuming, but some of you won't want it. Take a look at my recipe for Beautiful World Seasoning on page 51 for another great all-purpose seasoning without soy.

Onions, Scallions, Garlic, Shallots

All of these members of the Allium genus are somewhat carby, as vegetables go, but they're so flavorful and versatile that it's impossible to imagine cooking without them. I just watch the quantities.

When a recipe simply calls for an "onion," I'm talking about the common yellow onions you can buy in a net sack at any grocery store in America. Those are your all-purpose cooking onions. If you swap in a sweet onion, like a Vidalia or a red onion, you'll get a considerably milder flavor than if you use the common yellow variety.

On the other hand, those red onions, along with Vidalias and lovable little scallions, are mild and sweet, perfect for use in salads and other places you'll eat them raw. Again, swap in those yellow cooking onions, and you'll get a harsher flavor. Note that I have not actually called for Vidalias in any of these recipes; I like the color that red onions give to my dishes. But you can swap Vidalias for red onions if you like.

I buy fresh garlic two or three heads at a time; I couldn't keep house without it. Be aware that a garlic clove is one of those little segments that makes up the larger head of garlic. Use a whole head of garlic where I've called for a clove, and, well, your dish may be strong, but at least you won't have to worry about vampires.

I've grown quite fond of shallots, which occupy a botanical niche between onions and garlic. Look for them with the onions and garlic at your grocery store—they're bigger than garlic, usually smaller than onions and more teardrop shaped than round, and generally have reddish skins. Most shallots are made up of two segments inside a papery skin. When I call for "1 shallot," I'm talking about one of those segments, not both.

FYI: Refrigerated onions won't make you cry. Try it.

Hot Sauces

I am a bona fide chilehead and have an extensive collection of hot sauces, but there are only a few I have called for repeatedly in this book.

> **Tabasco:** The familiar original, this is a Louisiana-style hot sauce. Frank's or Louisiana brand will do fine as substitutes.

> **Frank's:** Another Louisiana-style hot sauce, Frank's is the canonical hot sauce used in the original Buffalo wings. As far as I'm concerned, that's enough reason to keep it on hand, but again, Tabasco or Louisiana will do.

> **Tabasco Chipotle:** A recent addition to the Tabasco family, Tabasco Chipotle has the smoky flavor expected of chipotles and a Tex-Mex, rather than Cajun, accent. Don't substitute regular Tabasco for this; you'd do better to go with another brand of chipotle hot sauce.

> **Sriracha:** This stuff is taking over the world. Starting as a specialty ingredient barely a decade ago, it's now everywhere. I use the original Huy Fong brand, with the rooster on the label. It's a must for Asian-style dishes but good in all sorts of things.

Soy Sauce

A word of warning for those of you who avoid gluten: Most soy sauce has wheat in it. I use San-J brand gluten-free soy sauce, which is widely available.

If you're avoiding all soy, coconut aminos are remarkably similar to soy sauce; look for them in health food stores or buy them online.

Nibbly Foods:
For Parties or Just For Fun

CHAPTER 1

These are the sorts of recipes we think of as party foods, but they are so filling that you may find yourself keeping one or two of these on hand so that you can have a quick snack in place of a whole meal. Remember, you're going to find yourself considerably less hungry than you're used to. It's really quite remarkable.

Olive, Cheese, and Bacon on a Stick! This is pretty self-explanatory.

It's a little fussy to stuff the tiny cheese cubes into the olives, but other than that, what's not to like?

2 ounces (55 g) Cheddar cheese

12 bacon slices

24 ripe pitted olives

Per serving: 33 calories; 3g fat (76.9% calories from fat); 2g protein; trace carbohydrate; trace dietary fiber

To assemble: Cut the cheese into 24 equal cubes. Cut the bacon strips in half.

Stuff a cube of cheese into each olive. Wrap with a half-slice of bacon, covering the cheese, and spear with a toothpick.

When party time rolls around, preheat the broiler. Arrange the skewers on the broiler rack and broil about 4 inches (10 cm) from the heat, turning once or twice, until the bacon is crisp. Drain on paper towels and serve hot.

Yield: 24 servings

Crispy Wings Okay, these only come to 63 percent fat on their own, hence my suggestion to serve them with Creamy Garlic Dip (page 56). Well, that's one reason; they're also yummy served that way. You'll be buying whole wings and cutting them in half; you could also buy pre-cut drumettes and wingettes.

½ cup (60 g) pork rind crumbs

½ cup (50 g) grated Parmesan cheese

1 tablespoon (7.5 g) Beautiful World Seasoning (page 51), or 1 teaspoon Vege-Sal or salt (but the umami in the Beautiful World or Vege-Sal really makes a difference)

1 tablespoon (7 g) hot paprika

⅓ cup (75 g) butter, melted

10 whole chicken wings, cut in half at the joints

Per piece: 76 calories; 5g fat (62.9% calories from fat); 7g protein; trace carbohydrate; trace dietary fiber

Preheat the oven to 350°F (180°C, or gas mark 4). Line a baking pan with aluminum foil.

On a rimmed plate, mix together the Pork Rind Crumbs, Parmesan, seasoning, and paprika.

On another rimmed plate, melt the butter. (I do this in the microwave, but hey, melt it in a pan on the stove and pour it onto a rimmed plate, if you prefer.)

Roll each chicken wing drumette in the butter, then in the coating mixture. Arrange on the foil.

Bake for 1 hour, basting gently at the 30-minute mark with the grease that will have gathered in the pan.

Yield: 20 pieces

Party Buffalo Wings

Traditionally, Buffalo wings are deep fried, then tossed with sauce, but man, who wants to do all that during a party? You can make these ahead, even the day before, and then just heat them through in the oven for about 10 minutes before serving. Try them with Blue Cheese Dip With Caramelized Shallots (page 55).

1 cup (225 g) butter, divided

1 cup (235 ml) Frank's hot sauce, divided (Oh, go ahead and use Tabasco or Louisiana brand if that's what you have, but Frank's is canonical.)

1 tablespoon (15 ml) Worcestershire sauce

1 teaspoon dried oregano

1 tablespoon (10 g) minced onion

1 clove of garlic, crushed

6 pounds (2.7 kg) whole chicken wings, cut in half at the joints

Blue cheese dressing, for serving

Per serving: 66 calories; 6g fat **(80.2% calories from fat)***; 3g protein; trace carbohydrate; trace dietary fiber*

Put ½ cup (112 g) of the butter and ½ cup (120 ml) of the hot sauce in a nonreactive saucepan over medium heat. Add the Worcestershire sauce, oregano, minced onion, and garlic and bring to a simmer. Turn the heat down a little and let it simmer for 5 minutes.

While this is happening, you have three tasks: Preheat the oven to 350°F (180°C, or gas mark 4), line 2 or 3 large roasting pans with aluminum foil (not essential, but it saves on cleanup), and put your wings into a large bowl.

Pour the sauce over the wings and toss till they're all evenly coated. Lay them in the roasting pans and stick 'em in the oven. After about 30 minutes, check on your wings. A good deal of fat will have gathered in the bottoms of the pans; spoon this over the wings and put them back in the oven for another 20 to 30 minutes.

Just before serving, melt the remaining ½ cup (112 g) butter with the remaining ½ cup (120 ml) hot sauce and brush the wings liberally with it. Serve with blue cheese dressing and plenty of napkins.

Yield: 50 servings

Bacon-Wrapped Artichokes and Mushrooms
This is an upscale version of mushroom bombs. The artichoke hearts add a little panache and a punch of flavor.

28 ounces (785 g) canned artichoke hearts, drained
4 ounces (115 g) mushrooms
1 pound (455 g) sliced bacon
½ cup (115 g) mayonnaise (see page 43)

Per serving: 478 calories; 40g fat (73% calories from fat); 21g protein; 12g carbohydrate; 6g dietary fiber

Cut the artichoke hearts in half. Cut the mushrooms into quarters. Pair up an artichoke heart half and a quartered mushroom with a slice of bacon, wrapping the two up into a bundle. Pierce the whole thing with a toothpick to secure. You can do this all ahead.

When it's time to cook, preheat the broiler. Arrange your bundles on your broiler rack and broil 6 inches (15 cm) from the heat, turning once or twice, till the bacon is crisp. Serve hot, with the mayonnaise for dipping.

NOTE: Aioli (page 44) would be good with these, too.

Yield: 8 servings

Deviled Eggs
Deviled eggs are hugely popular for parties and unironically retro, but they're also great to have in the fridge at any time, especially if you're fat fasting.

12 large eggs
⅔ cup (150 g) mayonnaise
1 tablespoon (15 g) brown mustard
1 teaspoon Tabasco sauce or other Louisiana-style hot sauce
Salt and ground black pepper, Vege-Sal, or Beautiful World Seasoning (page 51)
Paprika, for garnish

Per serving: 83 calories; 8g fat (83.2% calories from fat); 3g protein; trace carbohydrate; trace dietary fiber

Place the eggs in a pot in a single layer and add enough water to cover them by about 1 inch (2.5 cm). Bring the water to a boil and then remove from the heat and let the eggs sit in the water, covered, for about 12 minutes. Let cool.

Peel the eggs, cut them in half, and turn the yolks out into your food processor. (Yes, I have started using my food processor to mix deviled eggs; it makes them incomparably creamy.) Set the whites on a platter or in a big, flat snap-top container if you're planning to store/transport them.

Add the mayo, mustard, and Tabasco to the yolks. Run the processor, scraping down the sides a few times, until the mixture is completely creamy. Season with salt and pepper to taste.

Now, stuff the yolks into the whites. I like to spoon the yolks into my pastry bag and pipe them in using a star tip, but a spoon works just fine. Sprinkle with paprika and serve or refrigerate.

Yield: 24 servings

Avocado-Stuffed Eggs
My tester loved these and suggested putting a slice of ripe olive on each one. Don't make 'em ahead, though—you know how avocado turns brown.

12 large eggs, hard boiled

2 ripe avocados

2 tablespoons (28 g) mayonnaise

2 tablespoons (20 g) minced red onion

1 tablespoon (15 ml) lime juice

½ a clove of garlic, crushed

¼ teaspoon salt, or as needed

½ teaspoon Tabasco Chipotle sauce

Paprika, for garnish

Sliced ripe olives, for garnish

Minced fresh cilantro, for garnish

Per serving: 69 calories; 6g fat (73.1% calories from fat); 3g protein; 2g carbohydrate; trace dietary fiber

Peel your eggs and slice them in half, turning the yolks out into your food processor bowl. Set the whites aside.

Slice the avocados in half, remove the pits, scoop the innards of 1 avocado into the processor with those yolks, and add the mayo. Process, scraping down the sides as needed, until smooth.

Scrape into a bowl and add the flesh of the other avocado. Mash it in roughly—a whisk is good for this. Add the minced onion, lime juice, garlic, salt, and Tabasco and mash them in, too. Stuff the yolk-avocado mixture into the whites.

Sprinkle the eggs with paprika. If you'd like to be a little more decorative, add a slice of ripe olive, a little minced cilantro, or both.

Yield: 24 servings

Caesar Eggs
My tester Irysh said this recipe took 20 minutes, rated a 10, and adds, "We ate a *lot* of them and spoiled our dinner." It doesn't matter—these make a perfectly fine dinner.

12 large eggs, hard boiled

½ cup (115 g) mayonnaise

1½ tablespoons (23 g) brown mustard

2 teaspoons anchovy paste

1½ teaspoons lemon juice

½ teaspoon Worcestershire sauce

¼ cup (25 g) Parmesan cheese

2 tablespoons (8 g) minced fresh parsley

Per serving: 78 calories; 7g fat (78.8% calories from fat); 4g protein; trace carbohydrate; trace dietary fiber

Peel your eggs and halve them, turning the yolks out into your food processor. Set aside the whites. Add the mayonnaise, mustard, anchovy paste, lemon juice, and Worcestershire sauce to the yolks. Run the processor till the mixture is very smooth.

Stuff this mixture into the whites. Sprinkle the eggs with the Parmesan and parsley, and serve, or refrigerate till party time.

Yield: 24 servings

Sardine Eggs
Sardines have a lot going for them: They're full of omega-3 fatty acids, they're a great source of calcium, and because they're small and are lower on the food chain, they're unlikely to be contaminated with mercury. Add to that the fact that tinned sardines keep nicely in the pantry, and you can see that you need more sardine recipes.

6 large eggs, hard boiled

3¾ ounces (105 g) canned sardines in olive oil, drained

⅓ cup (75 g) mayonnaise

1 scallion

1 tablespoon (15 ml) lemon juice

1 teaspoon Worcestershire sauce

¼ teaspoon ground black pepper

Salt

Paprika, for garnish (I like smoked paprika here.)

Peel and halve your eggs, turning the yolks out into your food processor. Add the sardines, mayo, scallion, lemon juice, Worcestershire sauce, and pepper and run till it's getting smooth.

Taste for salt and add if needed, running the processor to mix it in.

Stuff the mixture into the whites; I like to use a pastry bag with a star tip, but it's not essential. Dust them lightly with paprika and serve.

Yield: 12 servings

Per serving: 102 calories; 9g fat (76.8% calories from fat); 5g protein; 1g carbohydrate; trace dietary fiber

Zesty Cheddar-Stuffed Celery
My tester Kim particularly liked the texture of this filling, but she suggested that you could gild the lily with a little crumbled bacon or minced jalapeño on top, if you want to take the trouble.

1 pound (455 g) sharp Cheddar cheese, shredded

2 ounces (55 g) cream cheese, softened

4 tablespoons (55 g) butter, softened

2 tablespoons (28 ml) dry sherry

2 teaspoons prepared horseradish

1 teaspoon Worcestershire sauce

14 large celery ribs

Run the Cheddar, cream cheese, butter, sherry, horseradish, and Worcestershire sauce through your food processor until well combined and then (surprise, surprise) stuff the mixture into the celery. Cut into 2- to 3-inch (5 to 7.5 cm) lengths to serve.

Yield: 56 servings

Per serving: 46 calories; 4g fat (76.2% calories from fat); 2g protein; 1g carbohydrate; trace dietary fiber

Chile-Lime Peanuts
Crunchy, a little spicy, with a Southwestern kick, these are super-tasty!

12 ounces (340 g) raw, shelled peanuts

1½ tablespoons (21 g) coconut oil, melted

1 tablespoon (15 ml) lime juice

½ teaspoon pure ground chile powder

½ teaspoon paprika (Smoked is great, but use what you have.)

⅛ teaspoon cayenne pepper

Salt

Per serving: 176 calories; 16g fat (74.4% calories from fat); 7g protein; 5g carbohydrate; 2g dietary fiber

Preheat the oven to 350°F (180°C, or gas mark 4). Line a jelly roll pan with aluminum foil.

Dump the peanuts onto the pan.

In a small dish, mix together the coconut oil, lime juice, chile powder, paprika, and cayenne.

Slowly pour the seasoning mixture over the peanuts, stirring the nuts constantly. Make sure they're all evenly coated.

Stick 'em in the oven and set the timer for 5 minutes. When it beeps, stir them again and put them back in the oven for another 5 minutes. Stir again and give them a final 5 minutes.

Sprinkle with salt to taste and let cool. Store in a tightly lidded container.

NOTE: My local grocery store carries raw Spanish peanuts (the ones with the red skins) in bags in the produce department. I can also find raw peanuts in the bulk section of my local health food store. Look around.

Yield: 12 servings

Spicy Pumpkin Seeds
Here's an even simpler, Louisiana-style recipe. I love pumpkin seeds, and they're a terrific source of minerals. They are cheaper than nuts, too. So here's something simple and savory to do with them.

¼ cup (56 g) coconut oil

2 cups (454 g) raw shelled pumpkin seeds

4 teaspoons (12 g) Creole seasoning

Per serving: 359 calories; 31g fat (71.5% calories from fat); 19g protein; 9g carbohydrate; 2g dietary fiber

Put your large skillet over medium-low heat and melt the coconut oil. Add the pumpkin seeds and stir until they puff a bit and start turning golden, maybe 5 to 6 minutes.

Stir in the Creole seasoning and remove from the heat. That's it!

NOTE: Look for shelled pumpkin seeds in the bulk section of your health food store, or in Mexican markets, where they will be labeled "pepitas."

Yield: 8 servings

Spicy-Sweet Spiced Pecans

These are devastatingly addictive. Put them out to impress the heck out of party guests or pass them as a sweet little nibble in lieu of dessert.

1 teaspoon salt

½ teaspoon ground cumin

½ teaspoon cayenne pepper

½ teaspoon ground cinnamon

½ teaspoon dried grated orange peel

1 pound (455 g) pecan halves

4 tablespoons (55 g) butter

¼ teaspoon liquid stevia (English toffee flavor)

2 tablespoons (28 ml) water

¼ cup (60 g) granular Swerve

Per serving: 126 calories; 13g fat (87.8% calories from fat); 1g protein; 3g carbohydrate; 1g dietary fiber

In a small dish, combine the salt, cumin, cayenne, cinnamon, and orange peel. Set aside.

In your large heavy skillet over medium-low heat, stir the pecan halves until they're smelling toasty, maybe 5 to 7 minutes.

Add the butter and melt it in, stirring often. While that's happening, add the stevia to the water.

When the pecans are thoroughly buttery, add the Swerve and stir it in; then stir in the water-stevia combo. Keep stirring till the water cooks away. Stir in the seasoning mixture.

Spread your pecans on waxed paper, baking parchment, or non-stick aluminum foil to cool. Store in a snap-top container for as long as you can keep them in the house. They tend to disappear.

Yield: 16 servings

Spiced Walnuts

English walnuts meet Asian seasonings. Imagine yourself on the terrace of the famous Raffles Hotel in Singapore when you serve these.

2 cups (200 g) walnut halves

2 tablespoons (30 g) granular Swerve

18 drops liquid stevia (English toffee flavor)

1 tablespoon (15 ml) soy sauce

2 teaspoons coconut oil, melted

½ teaspoon sriracha sauce

½ teaspoon smoked paprika

⅛ teaspoon cayenne pepper

Salt

Per serving: 201 calories; 19g fat (78.3% calories from fat); 8g protein; 4g carbohydrate; 2g dietary fiber

Preheat the oven to 325°F (170°C, or gas mark 3). Line a jelly roll pan with baking parchment.

Put your walnuts in a medium-size bowl. In a custard cup, mix together everything else but the salt. Pour this over the walnuts, and stir until they're evenly coated. Spread the nuts on the baking parchment in a single layer.

Put them in the oven and set the timer for 5 minutes. When it beeps, stir the nuts, spread them out again, and give them 5 minutes more. Stir again, spread them out again, and give them a final 5 minutes.

When they're crisp, season them lightly with salt while they're still hot, then let them cool on the parchment. Store in a snap-top container.

Yield: 8 servings

Mock Pâté
This makes a great party food served with celery or low-carb crackers. Celery stuffed with this yummy spread makes an easy take-along lunch. It's good in omelets, too.

8 ounces (225 g) braunschweiger (liverwurst)

3 ounces (85 g) cream cheese, softened

¼ cup (60 ml) heavy cream

1 tablespoon (14 g) butter, melted

1 tablespoon (15 ml) Worcestershire sauce

Salt and ground black pepper

Just put everything in your food processor and run till it's well combined. Heap it in a small, pretty dish and serve with your choice of accompaniments.

NOTE: At my grocery store, Oscar Mayer is the lowest-carb braunschweiger, but read the labels.

Yield: 6 servings

Per serving: 238 calories; 23g fat (85.4% calories from fat); 6g protein; 2g carbohydrate; trace dietary fiber

Cashew Chicken Dip
I love to scoop this with veggies! It's great for a party, of course, but it also makes a good lunch. Like every other leftover I find in my fridge, I use this in omelets, too. It is marvelous that way, especially with a little extra sriracha on top.

¾ cup (105 g) diced cooked chicken

2 scallions

¾ cup (175 g) mayonnaise

¼ cup (60 g) sour cream

1 tablespoon (15 ml) soy sauce

1 teaspoon grated fresh ginger

½ teaspoon sesame oil

¼ teaspoon sriracha sauce

1 clove of garlic, crushed

½ cup (70 g) roasted salted cashews

Put everything but the cashews in your food processor. Pulse until everything is pretty finely chopped and blended.

Add the cashews and pulse just enough to chop them up and distribute them, but not to pulverize them. You want recognizable bits of cashew in your dip.

Serve! If you have leftovers, store in a snap-top container in the fridge, but keep in mind that the cashews will soften.

Yield: 8 servings

Per serving: 241 calories; 24g fat (84.6% calories from fat); 6g protein; 4g carbohydrate; trace dietary fiber

Artichoke-Spinach Dip/Filling

Classically, this is served as a dip with crackers or vegetables, but I like to use it to stuff mushrooms (see next recipe), and I'll use any leftovers to fill omelets. It's super!

14 ounces (390 g) canned artichoke hearts, drained

3 scallions, cut into 1-inch (2.5 cm) lengths

8 ounces (225 g) cream cheese, softened

1 cup (100 g) grated Parmesan cheese

½ cup (115 g) mayonnaise

2 cloves of garlic, crushed

10 ounces (280 g) frozen chopped spinach, thawed and very well drained

This is so easy! Throw everything except the spinach in the food processor and pulse till the artichokes and scallions are chopped up. Add the spinach and run just long enough to blend it in, and you're done.

NOTE: If you want to serve this as a hot dip, spread it in a casserole dish, sprinkle the top with a little paprika, and bake for 45 to 50 minutes at 325°F (170°C, or gas mark 3).

Yield: 12 servings

Per serving: 182 calories; 16g fat (78.6% calories from fat); 6g protein; 4g carbohydrate; 1g dietary fiber

Artichoke-Spinach Stuffed Mushrooms

Here's that mushroom recipe I promised. It's excellent! Just don't pile the filling too high in the mushrooms, or your mushrooms may tip over while baking and make a mess. So says the Voice of Experience.

2 pounds (900 g) medium-size mushrooms (about 45)

Artichoke-Spinach Dip/Filling (above)

Paprika, for garnish

Per stuffed mushroom: 53 calories; 4g fat (71.6% calories from fat); 2g protein; 2g carbohydrate; trace dietary fiber

Preheat the oven to 325°F (170°C, or gas mark 3). Grease a 9 × 13-inch (23 × 33 cm) baking pan.

Remove the stems from your mushrooms. I like to save these to slice and sauté for other uses.

Stuff the mushrooms with the Artichoke-Spinach Dip/Filling. Be aware: I piled mine really high and had a few mushrooms invert themselves while baking. So fill 'em generously, but don't over-do it. As you fill your mushrooms, arrange them in your baking pan. When they're all full, sprinkle with paprika.

Give 'em 30 minutes in the oven and serve hot.

Yield: About 45 stuffed mushrooms

Peanut Hummus

Hummus is a hugely popular snack, but chickpeas are too carby and not high enough in fat for our purposes. Peanuts stand in nicely in this version of hummus. This is a little tricky to make, but it makes a lot and you can freeze it, so it's worth the extra time. You're not going to eat pita bread with this, but it's awfully good with cut-up veggies! You can serve pita wedges or chips for your friends, if you like.

12 ounces (340 g) raw shelled peanuts

¾ cup (175 ml) lemon juice (about 3 lemons)

⅔ cup (160 g) tahini

4 cloves of garlic, crushed, (more or less, depending on how big they are and how garlicky you like your hummus)

⅓ cup (80 ml) extra-virgin olive oil, plus more for serving

1 teaspoon ground cumin

⅓ cup (80 ml) water, or as needed

Salt

¼ cup (15 g) minced fresh parsley

Paprika, for garnish

Per serving: 204 calories; 19g fat (79% calories from fat); 6g protein; 6g carbohydrate; 2g dietary fiber

I'm afraid you need to start this ahead by peeling the skins off your peanuts. (If you can get raw peanuts without the skins, grab 'em! And if you're down South and can buy canned, boiled peanuts, this will be a snap.) Put the peanuts in a big saucepan, cover with water, and bring to a boil. All of 3 minutes later, pull them off the heat and drain them. This will loosen the skins, and most of them will come off with rubbing. The more diligent you are about peeling your peanuts, the creamier your hummus will be.

Okay, you've got a bunch of skinless, almost raw peanuts. Cover them with water again, bring to a boil and then turn down the burner and simmer for a good 3 to 4 hours until they're soft like any cooked legume, which is, of course, what they are. Drain them again. If you like, you can do this ahead and stash them in a snap-top container in the fridge for up to 5 days.

When the time comes to make the hummus, start by putting the lemon juice and tahini in your food processor. Let just these two ingredients process for 4 to 5 minutes before adding anything else. This apparently does something magical to improve the texture of your hummus.

Then add the boiled peanuts, garlic, olive oil, and cumin. Run the processor till the whole thing is finely ground. Now blend in the water; feel free to use a little more or less water to get the texture you like.

Season with salt to taste and then quickly blend in the parsley. It's done! This recipe makes quite a lot, so if you're not having a party, scrape it into a snap-top container and store it in the fridge. You can freeze it, too.

(continued on page 40)

Peanut Hummus
(continued from page 39)

When it's time to serve your hummus, spoon some into a dish, swirling it nicely. Dust it with a little paprika to make it look pretty and then pour some olive oil over the top.

NOTE: Tahini is sesame butter. Look for it in the grocery store with Middle Eastern and Asian foods.

Yield: 20 servings

Molded Shrimp Spread

My tester Rebecca says that this spread is rich enough, and makes so much, that it's really party food rather than an everyday dish. On the other hand, she says that the leftovers make a marvelous sauce melted over grilled or roasted salmon. Serve with cut-up vegetables and low-carb crackers.

6 ounces (170 g) cooked shrimp, without shells

1 tablespoon (1 envelope) unflavored gelatin

¾ cup (175 ml) boiling water

¼ cup (60 ml) lemon juice

¼ teaspoon liquid stevia (lemon drop flavor)

8 ounces (225 g) cream cheese, softened

1 cup (230 g) sour cream

½ cup (115 g) mayonnaise

⅓ cup (80 g) no-sugar-added ketchup

3 tablespoons (45 g) prepared horseradish

1 tablespoon (15 ml) white balsamic vinegar

2 teaspoons Worcestershire sauce

1 teaspoon Tabasco sauce

1 teaspoon dry mustard

Lettuce leaves, for serving

Oil a 5-cup (1 L) mold. Put your shrimp in the food processor and pulse till they're chopped to a medium consistency.

In a large measuring cup, dissolve the gelatin in the boiling water and then stir in the lemon juice and stevia.

In a medium bowl, beat the cream cheese until it's smooth. Beat in the sour cream, mayonnaise, ketchup, horseradish, vinegar, Worcestershire sauce, Tabasco, and dry mustard. Keep beating until everything is very well blended.

Beat in the gelatin mixture, incorporating it well. Stir in the chopped shrimp.

Pour the mixture into the prepared mold and chill until firm, a minimum of 5 hours, but overnight is better.

Unmold onto a lettuce-lined platter and serve with your choice of veggies and crackers.

Yield: 12 servings

*Per serving: 198 calories; 19g fat (**81.9% calories from fat**); 5g protein; 4g carbohydrate; trace dietary fiber*

Chicken Chips

Including this recipe is sort of cheating, because it's already in *500 Low-Carb Recipes*, but it's so good, and so easy, and so nutritious, that I had to throw it in again. Consider it a bonus.

Chicken skin (however much you
  have on hand)
Salt

Preheat the oven to 350°F (180°C, or gas mark 4). Spread the chicken skin flat on your broiler rack. Throw in any chunks of fat you might have on hand, too. Bake them until they're brown and crisp, at least 20 minutes. Salt them and stuff them in your face.

I have no way of knowing the exact nutrition count on these, since I can't find a listing for just chicken skin. Nor do I know how much of the fat in them cooks out, exactly. I know they're high in fat and also in gelatin, which is very good stuff. I have my local specialty butcher shop save me 10 pounds or so of skin at a time. (Here's a shout-out to The Butcher's Block in Bloomington, Indiana—you guys rock!) Then I freeze it in sandwich-size resealable plastic bags; one holds just about enough to cover the broiler rack.

Don't forget to pour the rendered chicken fat into a jar for cooking! That's schmaltz, one of the most beloved fats in Jewish cuisine.

Fat Snacks

Do you love the crispy fat on the edge of a steak or chop? Ask the nice butchers to save the fat they trim off meat—you know, to make low-fat steaks and chops for all those poor benighted souls who still want them. My butchers sell me fat trimmings for $1.99 a pound.

What do you do with that fat? Cut it into slices about ⅓ inch (1 cm) thick and lay them on your broiler rack. Bake at 350°F (180°C, or gas mark 4) until they've shriveled up and become brown and crispy. Season with salt, and devour.

By the way, you can do this with bits of ham skin, too, and it's outstanding. It's chewy, not for people with weak teeth, but outstanding.

Again, I have no way of knowing the exact nutrition count on these snacks because I don't know how much fat will cook out or what kind of fat you'll be using, but these goodies are definitely high in fat!

Sauces

CHAPTER 2

This may be the most important chapter in this book; it's certainly the most extensive. Despite what you may have heard, most cuts of meat are not so fatty that they derive 70 percent or more of their calories from fat. Neither are chicken or fish, and certainly most vegetables aren't. Sauces let you add fat while varying these menu staples. You can, of course, simply melt butter on things —not just steamed vegetables, but over steaks, eggs, or anything, really. I know people who bring coolers full of Kerrygold grass-fed butter on the Low-Carb Cruise to do exactly this.

But if you'd like some more variety, both in your fats and in flavor, this chapter contains a slew of ideas. Keep two or three of these sauces in the fridge at any time, and you'll be ready to add a hit of healthy fat and flavor to anything.

First comes mayonnaise because it's such a kitchen staple. Please try making mayonnaise.

It's really quick and easy, far quicker and easier than running to the store. Commercial mayonnaise is a Festival of Bad Oil. Even the "made with olive oil" kind is mostly cheap, nasty canola or soy oil.

If you're nervous about raw eggs, you can pasteurize them: Put your eggs in a saucepan and cover with water. Put them on a hot burner and bring the water to 140°F (60°C) (you'll need an instant-read thermometer). Maintain them at that temperature—no hotter or else you'll cook them—for 3 minutes. Then immediately pour off the hot water and rinse the eggs with several changes of cold water. Store in the refrigerator until needed or use right away. Me, I am unafraid of raw eggs. I personally think the danger is overblown because I've never gotten sick from a raw egg in my life. And anyway, did you ever refuse to lick cookie dough off a beater because of the raw egg in it? I didn't think so.

Mayonnaise As I Currently Make It
What do I mean by "as I currently make it?" Hey, my mayonnaise making evolves, you know? This is how I'm doing it right now. It takes less time to do it than it does to write about it.

1 large egg

1 egg yolk

1 tablespoon (15 ml) white wine vinegar

1 tablespoon (15 ml) lemon juice

1 teaspoon dry mustard

2 drops liquid stevia

½ teaspoon salt

2 dashes of Tabasco sauce

¾ cup (175 ml) light olive oil, Spectrum expeller-pressed sunflower oil, or MCT oil

¼ cup (56 g) coconut oil, melted

Per serving: 170 calories; 19g fat (97.7% calories from fat); 1g protein; trace carbohydrate; trace dietary fiber

Put the egg, egg yolk, vinegar, lemon juice, mustard, stevia, salt, and Tabasco in a food processor. (I use my little processor, but a blender is fine, too.) Have the oils mixed and standing by in a measuring cup with a pouring lip.

Run the food processor or blender for 20 seconds or so. Then, with the processor still running, slowly pour in the oils in a stream about the diameter of a pencil lead. When all the oil is in, it's done! Scrape it into a jar or snap-top container and stick it in the fridge.

NOTES: The coconut oil is to give the mayonnaise a somewhat stiffer consistency, since mayo made with all liquid oil is somewhat softer than commercial mayonnaise. Do use the bland stuff; if you use extra-virgin coconut oil you'll have coconut-flavored mayonnaise. By the way, you can also sub MCT oil for the olive oil if you want highly ketogenic mayonnaise.

If you use a lot of mayonnaise, feel free to double this recipe. Don't expect it to have the fridge life of the commercial stuff, though.

Yield: 1½ cups (340 g), or 12 servings

Aioli
This is a Mediterranean riff on mayonnaise—garlicky and delicious on artichokes, asparagus, fish, chicken, and stuff like that.

3 cloves of garlic, peeled

½ teaspoon salt

2 egg yolks

1 tablespoon (15 ml) lemon juice

1½ teaspoons Dijon mustard

1 cup (235 ml) oil (I suggest using half olive and half something blander)

Per serving: 172 calories; 19g fat **(97.7% calories from fat)**; *1g protein; trace carbohydrate; trace dietary fiber*

Put the garlic cloves and salt in your food processor and run till the garlic is pulverized.

Add the egg yolks, lemon juice, and mustard and run the processor till everything is well blended. Have the oil ready in a measuring cup with a pouring lip.

With the processor running, pour in the oil in a very thin stream, about the diameter of a pencil lead. When it's all in, it's done! Store in a lidded jar in the fridge.

NOTE: If you'd like to be all fancy, lightly steam and chill some asparagus. Arrange it in a spoke pattern on plates. Now put some aioli in a plastic bag, snip a teeny bit off the corner, and squeeze Jackson Pollock–like abstract patterns of sauce over each serving.

Yield: 1½ cups (340 g), or 12 servings

Lemon-Dill Mayonnaise
My tester Burma called this "super-easy" and said it was wonderful on grilled tuna and that "you'd never get anything this good at most restaurants."

1 large egg

1 egg yolk

1 teaspoon grated lemon zest

2 tablespoons (28 ml) lemon juice

¼ teaspoon dry mustard

¼ teaspoon salt

Dash of Tabasco sauce

½ a clove of garlic, crushed

1 cup (235 ml) light olive oil

1½ teaspoons minced fresh dill

1 teaspoon minced fresh parsley

Per serving: 258 calories; 28g fat **(97.5% calories from fat)**; *1g protein; 1g carbohydrate; trace dietary fiber*

Put the egg, egg yolk, lemon zest, lemon juice, dry mustard, salt, Tabasco, and garlic in your food processor and run for 20 seconds or so while you pour the oil into a measuring cup with a pouring lip.

With the processor running, slowly pour in the oil in a stream about the diameter of a pencil lead. When it's all worked in, add the dill and parsley, pulse till they're mixed in, and you're done. Store in a lidded jar in the fridge, of course.

Yield: 1 cup (225 g), or 8 servings

Chipotle Mayonnaise   Here's mayonnaise with a Southwestern accent.

1 large egg

1 egg yolk

2 canned chipotle chiles in adobo sauce

2 tablespoons (28 ml) lime juice

1 clove of garlic

¼ teaspoon ground cumin

¼ teaspoon salt

1 cup (235 ml) MCT, light olive oil, or sunflower oil. You can use part melted coconut oil, too.)

Put everything but the oil in your food processor and run it until the chipotle chiles are pulverized. While that's happening, pour the oil into a measuring cup with a pouring lip.

Leave the processor running and slowly pour in the oil in a stream about the diameter of a pencil lead. When all the oil is in, it's done! Put it in a jar and stash it in the fridge.

Yield: Generous 1 cup (225 g), or 8 servings

Per serving: 259 calories; 28g fat **(97% calories from fat)**; *1g protein; 1g carbohydrate; trace dietary fiber*

Mexican-ish Cheese Sauce   OMG. This is good over shirataki, cauliflower, Tex-Mex pulled pork, omelets, fingers—anything.

1 cup (235 ml) heavy cream

¾ cup (86 g) shredded Cheddar cheese

¾ cup (86 g) shredded Monterey Jack cheese

2 ounces (55 g) cream cheese, cut into small cubes

2 canned green chile peppers, minced

2 tablespoons (28 ml) liquid from chile peppers

½ cup (115 g) sour cream

In a heavy saucepan over medium-low heat, bring the cream to just below a simmer.

Whisk the Cheddar and Monterey Jack cheeses into the hot cream bit by bit; add only a couple of tablespoons (14 g) at a time, whisk till it's melted, and then add more. Whisk in the cream cheese. Don't let the sauce get quite hot enough to simmer!

Whisk in the chiles and their liquid. If you're making your sauce ahead, stop here and refrigerate; then reheat to just below a simmer right before serving, before you add the sour cream.

Right before serving, whisk in the sour cream. Let it get just hot through again—don't let it boil!—and serve.

NOTE: If you make this ahead, reheat it slowly, over low heat, and stop short of a simmer.

Yield: 8 servings

Per serving: 242 calories; 23g fat **(85.4% calories from fat)**; *7g protein; 2g carbohydrate; trace dietary fiber*

Provolone Sauce

Mixed with tofu shirataki, this makes an elegant mac and cheese, but also try it over Zoodles (page 95), cauliflower, or broccoli.

1 cup (235 ml) heavy cream

3 ounces (85 g) cream cheese

4 ounces (115 g) provolone cheese

⅛ teaspoon liquid smoke

¾ teaspoon salt

¼ teaspoon ground black pepper

3 dashes of Tabasco sauce or any Louisiana-style hot sauce

In a heavy saucepan over the lowest heat, warm the cream. When it's just below a simmer, whisk in the cream cheese. Tear the provolone into bits and whisk them in a little at a time, letting each piece melt before adding another.

Whisk in the liquid smoke, salt, pepper, and Tabasco, and it's done.

Yield: 1¾ cups (440 g), or 7 servings

Per serving: 217 calories; 21g fat (86.5% calories from fat); 6g protein; 2g carbohydrate; trace dietary fiber

Alfredo Sauce

This is rich and creamy, everybody's favorite, without the flour or cornstarch you find in the jarred sauces. Serve over shirataki, Zoodles (page 95), chicken, or shrimp. It's also a great addition to skillet suppers. Just sauté some diced chicken, a little onion, some mushrooms, and broccoli and then pour on the Alfredo. Dinner is served!

2 tablespoons (28 g) butter

2 cloves of garlic, crushed

¾ cup (175 ml) heavy cream

¾ cup (175 ml) half-and-half

1 ounce (28 g) cream cheese

1 cup (100 g) grated Parmesan cheese

2 tablespoons (8 g) minced fresh parsley

In a heavy saucepan over low heat, melt the butter. Add the garlic and sauté it for 4 to 5 minutes without browning it.

Add the cream and half-and-half and whisk them in. The butter will separate out a bit; do not panic. Let the whole thing come to a simmer.

Whisk in the cream cheese, stirring till it's melted. Then add the Parmesan, about ¼ cup (25 g) at a time. Keep whisking as the sauce smoothes out and thickens a bit.

Whisk in the parsley, and you're done.

Yield: 2½ cups (625 g), or 5 generous servings

Per serving: 306 calories; 29g fat (83.5% calories from fat); 9g protein; 4g carbohydrate; trace dietary fiber

Pesto
Okay, I admit it; this is not traditional pesto. But have you seen the price of pine nuts recently? Walnuts work wonderfully well. This pesto adds a hit of bright summer flavor to all sorts of things. Use the best-quality olive oil you can and freshly grate your Parmesan—it makes a big difference in this recipe.

2 packed cups (80 g) fresh basil leaves

¼ cup (25 g) walnuts

2 cloves of garlic, peeled

⅔ cup (160 ml) extra-virgin olive oil

½ cup (50 g) grated Parmesan cheese

Per serving: 139 calories; 14g fat **(92% calories from fat)**; *2g protein; 1g carbohydrate; trace dietary fiber*

Stuff your food processor with the basil, walnuts, and garlic. Turn it on and drizzle in the olive oil as it grinds.

When you've got an evenly mixed paste, add the Parmesan and run till it's worked in. That's it! Turn off the food processor, scrape your pesto into a clean glass jar, and stick it in the fridge or if you're not going to use it up quickly, the freezer.

NOTE: About that freshly grated Parmesan… before you start making pesto, run your block of Parmesan through the shredding blade of your food processor. Without removing the shreds from the work bowl, remove the disk and fit the S-blade down in there. Pulse till your cheese is finely grated. It's easy-peasy.

Yield: 1½ cups (390 g), or 12 servings

Lemon-Artichoke Pesto
The night I created this oh-so-simple pesto, I served it tossed with tofu shirataki noodles, but it would be delicious with chicken or fish, too.

14 ounces (395 g) canned artichoke hearts, drained

¾ cup (75 g) grated Parmesan cheese

¼ cup (60 ml) lemon juice

¼ cup (15 g) chopped fresh parsley

2 cloves of garlic, peeled

½ teaspoon salt

¼ teaspoon ground black pepper

½ cup (120 ml) extra-virgin olive oil

Per serving: 352 calories; 32g fat **(80% calories from fat)**; *9g protein; 9g carbohydrate; trace dietary fiber*

Put everything but the oil in your food processor. Run it for a minute or so. Then, with the processor running, pour in the oil. Check to see if it needs a little more salt (it will depend on your Parmesan), and you're done!

Yield: 2 cups (520 g), or 4 servings

Coconut Butter

At my health food store, coconut butter runs $12 a pound. Bulk shredded coconut runs $3 a pound, and it is the sole ingredient of coconut butter. If you're fond of coconut butter, this recipe will pay for a food processor by year's end.

4 cups (320 g) shredded coconut

Per serving: 142 calories; 13g fat
(80.2% calories from fat);
1g protein; 6g carbohydrate;
4g dietary fiber

Super-simple: Dump the coconut in your food processor with the S-blade in place, and turn it on. Set your timer for 20 minutes, and go do something else. Come back and scrape the coconut butter into a snap-top container!

NOTE: The fresher the coconut, the better this will work. Find a store with brisk turnover.

Yield: 1 cup, or 8 servings

Anchovy-Shallot Butter

This is simple, classic, and perfect over steak. If you're skeptical, just remember that Worcestershire sauce contains anchovies.

10 tablespoons (140 g) butter, softened
¼ cup (40 g) minced shallot (about 1)
2 anchovy fillets
1 tablespoon (4 g) minced fresh parsley

Per serving: 106 calories; 12g fat
(95.7% calories from fat);
trace protein; 1g carbohydrate;
trace dietary fiber

In a medium-size skillet over medium low heat, melt 2 tablespoons (28 g) of the butter, and sauté the shallot until it's soft and golden.

Transfer the shallot and melted butter to the food processor and add the rest of the butter and the anchovy fillets. Process until the anchovies disappear. Add the parsley and pulse till it's mixed in.

If you want to be classical about this, turn the mixture out onto a piece of plastic wrap and form into a roll maybe 1½ inches (3.8 cm) in diameter. Wrap it up and chill. Then slice pretty round pats to melt over steaks. If that sounds like too much trouble, just keep it in a snap-top container and scoop it out by the spoonful. It's going to melt anyway, you know.

Yield: 10 servings

Maître d'Hôtel Butter

This is a classic sauce, so versatile, and one of the secrets of top-notch steak houses. Consider the secret revealed.

½ cup (112 g) butter, softened

2 teaspoons lemon juice

1 tablespoon (4 g) minced fresh parsley

Per serving: 102 calories; 11g fat **(98.9% calories from fat);** *trace protein; trace carbohydrate; trace dietary fiber*

Put the butter in your food processor and run till it's creamy. Add the lemon juice and run till it's evenly blended in. Add the parsley and pulse just till it's mixed in; you don't want to pulverize it.

If you make this ahead of time, you can scrape it out onto a piece of plastic wrap, form it into a tidy roll, and stash it in the fridge. Then you can slice pretty pats of it to melt on your steaks. It's not only tasty, but also impressive, should you have anyone you'd like to impress.

Yield: 8 servings

Maple Butter

Here's a great alternative to sugar-free pancake syrup, with all of that great maple flavor and none of the carbs. This also does miraculous things to roasted root vegetables. Look for natural maple flavoring rather than artificial.

½ cup (112 g) butter, softened

⅛ teaspoon maple flavoring

About 20 drops liquid stevia (English toffee flavor)

Per serving: 102 calories; 11g fat **(99.5% calories from fat);** *trace protein; trace carbohydrate; 0g dietary fiber*

Just put everything in the food processor and run till it's all combined.

Yield: 8 servings

Kansas City Barbecue Sauce

This sauce is easy and delicious, but if you want to cheat, Stubb's brand barbecue sauce is considerably lower in sugar than most of the commercial barbecue sauces on the market, and it's awfully good.

1 tablespoon (14 g) butter

1 clove of garlic, crushed

¼ cup (40 g) minced onion

1 cup (240 ml) no-sugar-added ketchup

¼ cup (30 g) powdered erythritol

1 tablespoon (20 g) blackstrap molasses

¼ teaspoon liquid stevia (English toffee flavor)

2 tablespoons (28 ml) Worcestershire sauce

1 tablespoon (15 ml) white vinegar

1 tablespoon (15 ml) lemon juice

1 tablespoon (8 g) chili powder

1 teaspoon ground black pepper

¼ teaspoon salt

Put a good-size, heavy, nonreactive saucepan over low heat. Melt the butter and sauté the garlic and onion until they soften, taking care not to brown them.

Add everything else. Bring to a simmer and let it all cook for 20 to 30 minutes.

Stash it in a snap-top container and use it like any barbecue sauce.

Yield: Generous 1½ cups (375 g), or 14 servings

Per serving: 21 calories; 1g fat (38.4% calories from fat); trace protein; 3g carbohydrate; trace dietary fiber

Beautiful World Seasoning

Okay this isn't a sauce but it *is* one of the best things I've ever come up with. Why? Because both shiitake mushrooms and kelp are loaded with umami—free glutamates—and therefore are natural flavor enhancers. I've taken to putting this in or on everything—really, if it's not sweet, this will improve it.

½ ounce (15 g) dried shiitake mushrooms

2 tablespoons (13 g) celery seeds

2 tablespoons (14 g) onion powder

2 tablespoons (18 g) garlic powder

1 tablespoon (12 g) granular kelp seaweed

½ cup (150 g) salt (I use high-quality, mined, ancient seabed sea salt.)

Per serving: 4 calories; trace fat (14.9% calories from fat); trace protein; 1g carbohydrate; trace dietary fiber

First break up the mushrooms and grind them to a powder in your food processor. This will create a regrettable quantity of dust; I had to actually brush some up and put it back in the processor.

Add the celery seeds, grind for another minute, and then add everything else and grind till it's well blended. Run through a strainer to remove any stray lumps of mushroom (you can save these for the next batch). Store the seasoning in an old spice shaker.

NOTE: You can get granular kelp at the health food store, or, no doubt, on Amazon.com, like everything else in the world.

Yield: 1 cup (120 g), or 48 servings

Cocoyo and Coconut Sour Cream

Coconut milk can be cultured, just like dairy milk, to make yogurt, or "Cocoyo." Simply pour a can of coconut milk into a clean snap-top container and add either a dollop of already-existing yogurt, an envelope of purchased yogurt culture, or the contents of a good-quality probiotic capsule. Whisk it in well. Cover and put in a warm place—I use an electric heating pad set on low, tucked down in a bowl, and cover the whole thing with a tea towel. Let it sit for 12 hours or so, then refrigerate and use in place of yogurt.

For "sour cream," refrigerate your can of coconut milk overnight. Then turn it upside down, poke two holes, one on either side of the rim, and pour off the liquid. Open the can; scrape out the concentrated cream and culture like Cocoyo. For that matter, I have occasionally had a batch of Cocoyo separate. If this happens, pour off the liquid and use the rest as sour cream.

Be aware that sometimes Cocoyo looks gray and unappetizing at first, but improves greatly with overnight refrigeration.

Hollandaise Sauce

I've published a recipe for blender hollandaise before, but it's such a rich and classic sauce that this book wouldn't be complete without it. Serve over broccoli, asparagus, eggs, or anything.

½ cup (112 g) butter or ghee (Some recipes recommend the ghee.)

4 egg yolks

½ teaspoon salt

1 tablespoon (15 ml) lemon juice

2 dashes of Tabasco sauce, or as needed

Per serving: 264 calories; 28g fat **(94.5% calories from fat)**; *3g protein; 1g carbohydrate; trace dietary fiber*

In a small saucepan over low heat, melt the butter. Be careful here—you need to get it just to the bubbling point, but you can't let it brown. If you like, you can use ghee instead, which doesn't have milk solids in it to burn.

While the butter is melting, put the yolks, salt, lemon juice, and Tabasco in your blender or food processor (I use my little food processor for this; it's not enough stuff for the big one.) Run the blender till it's all well combined.

Go check your butter!

When your butter has just reached the bubbling point, turn the blender back on. Take the knob out of the blender lid so you can pour through the lid. With the blender running, slowly pour in the butter in a thin, continuous stream, about the diameter of a pencil lead.

When all the butter is worked in and the sauce is thick and fluffy, you're done! Grab your asparagus—or whatever.

NOTE: The trick here is to have the butter hot enough. If it's just melted but not bubbling hot, your sauce won't thicken properly.

Yield: 4 servings

Béarnaise Sauce
This is a "child" of the "mother sauce" hollandaise, with the addition of shallot and tarragon. It's also a classic, especially over steak.

¼ cup (60 ml) dry white wine
¼ cup (60 ml) tarragon vinegar
1 tablespoon (4 g) fresh tarragon leaves
1 tablespoon (10 g) minced shallot
2 egg yolks
½ cup (112 g) butter, cut into pieces

*Per serving: 247 calories; 26g fat **(94.5% calories from fat)**; 2g protein; 2g carbohydrate; 0g dietary fiber*

In a small saucepan over low heat, reduce the wine to about 1 tablespoon (150 ml). Put it in the top of a double boiler, along with the tarragon vinegar, fresh tarragon, minced shallot, and egg yolks. Have your butter ready.

Okay, it's showtime: Put the double boiler over simmering water. Turn on your stick blender and immerse it in the egg yolks and seasonings and blend everything up.

Keep blending! Start adding the butter 1 to 1½ tablespoons (14 to 21 g) at a time, blending the whole time. Keep blending for about 30 seconds between each addition of butter.

Your sauce should start thickening and fluffing up. Keep blending!

When all the butter is in, keep blending for another minute or two, making sure your sauce is good and thick before you turn off the stick blender and take it off the heat. If it's not finished cooking, your sauce will fall apart.

Any leftovers will keep for a day or two in a snap-top container in the fridge.

NOTES: I happen to keep my small slow cooker, lidless, full of water, set to low, on my kitchen counter during the winter; it makes an effective humidifier. I set a steel mixing bowl down into the slow cooker and used it as a double boiler. It worked great! If you don't have hot water already in the slow cooker, you could warm some on the stovetop, pour it into your slow cooker, and proceed from there. Or just use a double boiler.

Or you could take the easy route and make it the way you would make the blender hollandaise on page 52. I just thought I'd try the classical route for a change.

Yield: 4 servings

Horseradish Sauce

This is quick and easy and killer on any kind of beef! I've made this with Coconut Sour Cream (page 51) instead of regular, and that worked well, too.

½ cup (115 g) sour cream
¼ cup (60 g) mayonnaise
2 tablespoons (30 g) prepared horseradish
2 teaspoons cider vinegar
1 teaspoon dry mustard
¼ teaspoon Tabasco sauce

Just mix it all together. That's it! Store any leftovers in the fridge, of course.

Yield: ¾ cup (175 g), or 6 servings

Per serving: 111 calories; 12g fat ***(91.9% calories from fat)****; 1g protein; 2g carbohydrate; trace dietary fiber*

Brown Sauce

This is great over beef, of course, but how about with sautéed mushrooms over Mixed Mashed fauxtatoes (page 95)? Or over shirataki? You could use it to turn bits of leftover roast beef or a pan full of browned and crumbled hamburger into a meal, too.

2 tablespoons (28 g) butter
1 tablespoon (10 g) minced shallot
1½ cups (355 ml) beef stock
¼ cup (60 ml) dry red wine
Pinch of dried thyme
2 ounces (55 g) cream cheese
Guar or xanthan, as needed
Salt and ground black pepper

In a small, heavy saucepan over medium heat, melt the butter. Sauté the shallot in the butter until it's softened.

Add the beef stock, wine, and thyme and turn the heat up a bit, till it's simmering. Let it cook down to 1 cup (225 g); this will take about 20 minutes.

Melt in the cream cheese. Now use the guar or xanthan shaker to thicken it a bit more to your liking. Season with salt and pepper to taste.

NOTE: You can make this with chicken stock and white wine for a sauce similar to velouté.

Yield: 1 cup (240 g), or 4 servings

Per serving: 121 calories; 11g fat ***(89.3% calories from fat)****; 2g protein; 1g carbohydrate; trace dietary fiber*

Buffalo Sauce

This super-easy recipe is what gave rise to the Great Buffalo Wing Concept. You'll never buy bottled Buffalo sauce again. Frank's hot pepper sauce is canonical here, but Louisiana hot sauce or Tabasco will work, too.

½ cup (112 g) butter
1 clove of garlic, crushed
½ cup (120 ml) hot pepper sauce

Per 1 cup: 830 calories; 92g fat (97.8% calories from fat); 2g protein; 3g carbohydrate; 1g dietary fiber

Melt the butter with the garlic in a small saucepan and then stir in the hot sauce. This is sum total of recipe. Now pour over wings and toss. Add blue cheese dressing, and a stack of napkins!

NOTE: Traditionally Buffalo wings are deep fried, and often floured first, too. Instead, just roast them until crisp, and toss them with the sauce. It's much easier, just as good, and there's no fryer oil to dispose of.

Yield: 1 cup (235 ml)

Blue Cheese Dip with Caramelized Shallots

I first made this to go with the Party Buffalo Wings (page 31) for my Toastmasters Christmas Bash. It's great on burgers and steaks or with cut-up veggies, too.

¼ cup (40 g) minced shallot
1½ tablespoons (23 g) bacon grease
⅔ cup (150 g) mayonnaise
⅔ cup (155 g) sour cream
½ cup (60 g) crumbled blue cheese
2 dashes of hot pepper sauce
Salt and ground black pepper

Per serving: 152 calories; 16g fat (92.3% calories from fat); 2g protein; 1g carbohydrate; trace dietary fiber

In a small, heavy skillet over medium-low heat, sauté the shallots in the bacon grease until they're golden brown.

Put the mayo, sour cream, blue cheese, and hot pepper sauce into a bowl, add the shallot, and mix it up. Season with salt and pepper to taste. Store in a clean glass jar (score irony points for using one from commercial blue cheese dressing).

Yield: 2 cups (480 g), or 12 servings

Creamy Garlic Dip

Obviously, you can serve this with cut-up vegetables, but it's a tasty topping for meat or poultry as well.

2 tablespoons (28 g) butter

4 cloves of garlic, crushed

½ cup (115 g) sour cream

½ cup (115 g) mayonnaise

2 tablespoons (8 g) minced fresh parsley

1 teaspoon Worcestershire sauce

½ teaspoon salt

¼ teaspoon ground black pepper

In a small skillet over low heat, melt the butter and sauté the garlic, taking care not to brown it. It just needs a few minutes.

Scrape into a bowl, add everything else, and stir it all up. That's it! This is best if you chill it for several hours to let the flavors marry, but I confess that I haven't always taken the time.

Yield: 8 servings

Per serving: 158 calories; 18g fat (95% calories from fat); 1g protein; 1g carbohydrate; trace dietary fiber

Walnut Sauce

This is insanely rich and awfully good. I like to toss shirataki angel hair with this; I'd use two packets of shirataki, drained, microwaved, and drained again, for this much sauce. Usually, I consider a packet of shirataki to be one serving, but with a sauce this rich, half a packet per customer is plenty. Oh, and this sauce would also be brilliant over chicken!

1 cup (100 g) walnuts

½ cup (120 ml) heavy cream

½ cup (50 g) grated Parmesan cheese

⅓ cup (80 ml) extra-virgin olive oil

1 clove of garlic, peeled

2 tablespoons (8 g) minced fresh parsley

½ teaspoon salt

¼ teaspoon ground black pepper

Preheat the oven to 350°F (180°C, or gas mark 4). Spread the walnuts on a shallow baking pan, transfer to the oven, and set your timer for 8 minutes.

In the meanwhile, put the cream, Parmesan, oil, garlic, parsley, salt, and pepper in the food processor with the S-blade in place.

When the walnuts are toasted, add them to the stuff in the food processor, run the processor till you have a thick paste, and you're done! You may heat it gently on the stovetop or in the microwave, if you'd like it warm.

Yield: 4 servings

Per serving: 470 calories; 47g fat (87.9% calories from fat); 8g protein; 6g carbohydrate; 1g dietary fiber

Vodka Sauce

This traditional Italian pasta sauce is always made with cream, so it's a natural for us. Serve over shirataki or Zoodles (page 95).

¼ cup (57 g) butter

3 tablespoons (30 g) diced onion

⅓ cup (80 ml) vodka

1 can (8 ounces, or 225 ml) tomato sauce

1 cup (235 ml) heavy cream

Pinch of red pepper flakes (optional)

In a medium-size saucepan over low heat, melt the butter. Sauté the onion in the butter until it's soft.

Add the vodka and tomato sauce. Bring to a simmer, and let it cook for 10 minutes.

Stir in the heavy cream and red pepper flakes, if desired. Bring it back to a low simmer, let it cook for another 5 minutes or so, and it's done.

NOTE: Most of the alcohol will cook off while it simmers, but I can't guarantee there will be no residual booze.

Per serving: 185 calories; 17g fat (89.8% calories from fat); 1g protein; 3g carbohydrate; trace dietary fiber

Yield: 2 cups (490 g), or 8 servings

Remoulade Sauce

This is an old classic with seafood. Serve it with crab, shrimp, crawfish, or, really, anything that lived in the water.

4 scallions

4 cloves of garlic, peeled

¼ cup (30 g) diced celery

¼ cup (15 g) chopped fresh parsley

¼ cup (60 g) no-sugar-added ketchup

2 tablespoons (30 g) brown mustard

2 tablespoons (22 g) yellow mustard

4 teaspoons (20 g) prepared horseradish

⅛ teaspoon cayenne pepper

⅛ teaspoon ground black pepper

Just put everything in your food processor and run it till the scallions, celery, garlic, and parsley are pulverized. Store in a snap-top container in the fridge.

Yield: 1½ cups (355 ml), or 6 servings

Per serving: 179 calories; 19g fat (90.1% calories from fat); 1g protein; 3g carbohydrate; 1g dietary fiber

Roasted Red Pepper Sauce

I like this on shirataki, but That Nice Boy I Married thinks it's phenomenal with shrimp. How about with shirataki *and* shrimp? It would be good on fish fillets, too, and, of course, on Zoodles (page 95).

3 ounces (85 g) jarred roasted red peppers, drained and patted dry

3 tablespoons (45 g) Pesto (page 47, or purchased pesto)

1 clove of garlic, peeled

Pinch of red pepper flakes (optional)

1 cup (235 ml) heavy cream

2 tablespoons (10 g) grated Parmesan cheese

Salt and ground black pepper

Guar or xanthan (optional)

Put the roasted red peppers in your food processor along with the pesto, garlic, and red pepper flakes, if using, and run the processor till the whole thing is a uniform paste. Scrape this mixture into a small, heavy saucepan and set over low heat.

Whisk in the cream and bring the whole thing to a simmer. Whisk in the Parmesan and season with salt and pepper to taste. Thicken it up a little with the guar or xanthan shaker, if you like, but go easy.

This will keep for at least a few days in the fridge, and it warms up nicely in the microwave.

Yield: 1½ cups (360 g), or 5 servings

Per serving: 224 calories; 22g fat (88.1% calories from fat); 3g protein; 3g carbohydrate; trace dietary fiber

Lemon Olive Oil

I've seen involved recipes for infusing olive oil with lemon zest, but this is far simpler and yields terrific results. Drizzle over chicken or fish or use for salad dressings or sautéing vegetables.

1 cup (235 ml) extra-virgin olive oil

10 drops lemon essential oil

Mix 'em together and store in a glass bottle in the refrigerator. That's it.

Yield: 16 servings

Per serving: 119 calories; 14g fat (100% calories from fat); 0g protein; 0g carbohydrate; 0g dietary fiber

Thousand Barbecue Dressing

Why is it called "Thousand Barbecue"? Because instead of the ketchup in standard Thousand Island dressing, this version uses no-sugar-added barbecue sauce instead. See the recipe on page 50, or use any one of the barbecue sauce recipes I've previously published.

½ cup (115 g) mayonnaise

2 tablespoons (32 g) no-sugar-added barbecue sauce (see page 50)

1 tablespoon (15 g) minced sugar-free bread-and-butter pickles (You can find these with the other pickles)

1 teaspoon cider vinegar

1 teaspoon minced onion

Salt and ground black pepper

Just stir everything together! Great on burgers.

Yield: ⅓ cup (85 g), or 6 servings

Per serving: 136 calories; 16g fat **(96.9% calories from fat)**; *trace protein; 1g carbohydrate; trace dietary fiber*

Mushroom Sauce

How many recipes do you shy away from because they call for starchy canned cream of mushroom soup? Here's your alternative. This will work in almost any casserole that calls for canned mushroom soup.

2 tablespoons (28 g) beef fat or butter

4 ounces (115 g) mushrooms, chopped

2 tablespoons (20 g) minced onion

½ cup (120 ml) beef broth

¾ cup (175 ml) heavy cream

½ teaspoon xanthan, guar, or glucomannan

In a saucepan over medium-low heat, melt the beef fat. Sauté the mushrooms and onion in the fat until they're soft. Add the beef broth, bring to a simmer, and let it cook for 5 minutes.

Whisk in the cream and xanthan, let it heat through and thicken, and it's done.

NOTE: Thin this out with more beef broth, and you've got a good mushroom soup.

Yield: 1½ cups (360 g), or 4 servings

Per serving: 228 calories; 23g fat **(89.1% calories from fat)**; *3g protein; 3g carbohydrate; trace dietary fiber*

Baked Goods, "Cereals," and Other Grainlike Things

This is a shorter chapter than some of the others. Quite honestly, having eaten way I do for almost 20 years—over 30 percent of my life now—I just don't miss baked goods, cereals, and other grain-based products that much. Still, every now and then these make a nice change or satisfy a yen.

Coconut Flax Bread

This is reprinted from *The Fat Fast Cookbook* by permission of my friends at CarbSmart. Very simply, this bread recipe was just too good not to include. I know it sounds odd, but it's surprisingly, well, bread-like. It's grain-free, gluten-free, and delicious! Buttered toast is a staple again in my house.

4 cups (320 g) shredded coconut

¾ cup (84 g) flaxseed meal

1 tablespoon (9 g) xanthan or guar

1 teaspoon erythritol (It's not essential, but I think it improves the flavor.)

1½ teaspoons baking soda

½ teaspoon salt

½ cup (120 ml) water

2 tablespoons (28 ml) cider vinegar

4 large eggs

Per serving: 111 calories; 9g fat (69.9% calories from fat); 4g protein; 5g carbohydrate; 4g dietary fiber

Preheat the oven to 350°F (180°C, or gas mark 4). Grease a standard-size loaf pan—mine is 4½ × 8½ inches (11 × 21 cm)—line it with nonstick aluminum foil or baking parchment.

In your food processor with the S-blade in place, combine the coconut, flaxseed meal, xanthan, erythritol, baking soda, and salt. Run the processor till everything is ground to a fine meal. Scrape down the sides and run the processor some more.

In a glass measuring cup, combine the water and the vinegar. Have this standing by the food processor.

With the food processor still running, add the eggs, one at a time, through the feed tube. Finally, pour the water and vinegar mixture in through the feed tube. Run for just another 30 seconds or so.

Pour or scrape the batter into the prepared loaf pan. Bake for 1 hour 15 minutes. Turn the bread out onto a wire rack to cool. This slices beautifully and can be sliced thick or thin. I get about 20 slices per loaf.

Yield: 20 servings

Almond Butter Pancakes

So there I was on a Sunday morning with a jar of almond butter. Guess what happened? These came out remarkably well, and making the batter in the blender was a snap. Serve with Maple Butter (page 49) or plain butter and low-sugar preserves.

¾ cup (195 g) almond butter

3 large eggs

¼ cup (60 ml) heavy cream

2 tablespoons (28 ml) water

1½ teaspoons baking powder

⅛ teaspoon salt

¼ cup (56 g) coconut oil

Heat your griddle or large heavy skillet over medium heat; you'll want it to be hot before you start cooking.

Put everything but the coconut oil in your blender and run it until you have a smooth batter.

(continued on page 62)

Almond Butter Pancakes

(continued from page 61)

Per serving: 202 calories; 19g fat
(81.3% calories from fat); 6g protein;
4g carbohydrate; 2g dietary fiber

Cook just like any pancakes. You'll want the first side to be well browned before you try to flip them. I cooked mine in my biggest nonstick skillet, but added the coconut oil, a spoonful at a time, to fry 'em in.

Yield: 10 servings

Flax and Coconut Pancakes

These are so tasty and so, so filling! I challenge you to eat more than two—or to be hungry again within several hours. I love mine with butter, Polaner low-sugar, high-fiber preserves, and a side of bacon.

½ cup (56 g) flaxseed meal

½ cup (40 g) shredded coconut

½ teaspoon baking soda

½ teaspoon salt

½ cup (115 g) sour cream or
   Coconut Sour Cream (page 51)

3 large eggs

¼ teaspoon liquid stevia (English
   toffee flavor), as needed

Per serving: 141 calories; 11g fat
(67.8% calories from fat); 6g protein;
6g carbohydrate; 5g dietary fiber

Heat your griddle or large skillet over medium-high heat. Get it hot before you add the wet ingredients to the dry ones! Once you do that, you want to be ready to cook.

In a large bowl, combine the flaxseed meal, shredded coconut, baking soda, and salt. Stir them all together until evenly distributed.

Measure the sour cream into a 2-cup (475 ml) measure, then add the eggs and stevia, and whisk it all together. Dump this into the dry ingredients and whisk it up till it's smooth.

Scoop the batter onto the griddle by a ¼-cup (60 ml) measure and fry like any pancakes. You'll want the first side to be well browned before you try to flip them. I cooked mine in a big nonstick skillet, but added coconut oil to the pan for good measure. Lard or bacon grease would work well, too.

NOTE: This batter is quite thick and makes thick pancakes—they rise to about ¾ inch (2 cm). I like them that way, but you can thin the batter with a bit of water or cream, if you like.

Yield: 8 servings

Baked Breakfast Pudding
If you have some, a handful of sugar-free chocolate chips would be really nice in this! See the Notes that follow for a bunch of additional serving suggestions for this lovely pudding.

⅓ cup (27 g) shredded coconut

3 tablespoons (21 g) flaxseed meal

1 teaspoon chia seeds

⅛ teaspoon salt

¼ cup (60 ml) water

⅓ cup (80 ml) unsweetened coconut milk

3 tablespoons (42 g) coconut butter, melted (see page 48)

12 drops liquid stevia (English toffee flavor), as desired

1 teaspoon vanilla extract

Per serving: 733 calories; 66g fat (75.3% calories from fat); 16g protein; 32g carbohydrate; 24g dietary fiber

Preheat the oven to 350°F (180°C, or gas mark 4) and grease a 10-ounce (285 ml) ramekin.

In a bowl, combine the coconut, flaxseed meal, chia seeds, and salt, stirring them together. Stir in the water and let the whole thing stand for 10 minutes to thicken.

In the meanwhile, in a bowl, combine the coconut milk, coconut butter, stevia, and vanilla.

When the dry ingredients have soaked up all the water and softened a bit, stir in the wet ingredients, making sure to combine everything well.

Pour the pudding into the prepared ramekin and bake for 15 minutes or so. Serve hot.

NOTES: My testers had a lot of good suggestions for this.

Tammera suggests that you throw this together in the evening and then simply microwave it to heat it through in the morning. She also said that this is a big serving—right for breakfast, but that halving it would make a good dessert portion. Oh, and that the toffee stevia was delicious, but she thinks vanilla stevia would be good, too, or a fruit flavor, or cinnamon. She ate the leftovers cold, straight out of the fridge, and called it a "refreshing snack or dessert," especially for summertime.

Valerie says that at 8 grams of usable carbs, this is too high for her to eat for breakfast regularly, but that she really liked it and would eat it as an occasional alternative. She also suggested that you could mix up the dry ingredients in advance and that you could add any extract you like to vary this. Valerie used 2 heaping teaspoons of granular xylitol in place of the stevia.

Burma says her husband "absolutely loved this" with a little cream and some slivered almonds on top. She suggests a pumpkin version, though that will add a few carbs.

Yield: 1 serving

63

Chocolate-Hazelnut Hot "Cereal"
Here's a yummy hot breakfast, quick and easy! You can skip the vanilla whey protein if you like, which will up the fat percentage, but I think it keeps me full longer.

3 tablespoons (15 g) shredded coconut

2 tablespoons (14 g) almond meal

4 teaspoons (9 g) flaxseed meal

1 tablespoon (8 g) vanilla whey protein powder

3 tablespoons (56 g) Chocolate-Hazelnut Spread (page 179)

⅓ cup (80 ml) boiling water

3 tablespoons (45 ml) heavy cream

In a bowl, combine the coconut, almond meal, flaxseed meal, and vanilla whey protein powder, stirring them together. Plunk the Chocolate-Hazelnut Spread on top.

Add the boiling water and stir it all up till the spread melts and blends in to the mixture.

Add the cream and serve!

Yield: 1 serving

Per serving: 573 calories; 48g fat (69.9% calories from fat); 26g protein; 20g carbohydrate; 10g dietary fiber

Chia Breakfast Custard
Highly nutritious, low in carbs, and loaded with fiber, chia seeds are all the rage in health food circles. They give custards and puddings a texture similar to tapioca. I add a handful of sugar-free chocolate chips to my custard, but that's up to you. A drizzle of sugar-free pancake syrup might be nice or a dusting of ground cinnamon.

2 tablespoons (26 g) chia seeds

½ cup (120 ml) water

¼ cup (60 ml) heavy cream

1 egg yolk

Liquid stevia (vanilla, English toffee, or whatever flavor you like), as needed

Pinch of salt

This recipe turns on one simple act of forethought: The evening before you want to eat this, put the chia seeds in a serving bowl and stir in the water. Stick the bowl in the fridge and go to bed.

Okay, it's morning. Grab a cup of coffee or tea and pull your chia seeds out of the fridge. Stir them up with a fork to break up any clumps.

Pour the cream into a glass measuring cup and add the egg yolk. Use the fork to stir the cream and the egg yolk together quite well. Stir in the stevia and the salt; I like to use 10 drops each of French vanilla (NOW brand) and English toffee (SweetLeaf brand).

Per serving: 408 calories; 36g fat (77.8% calories from fat); 9g protein; 14g carbohydrate; 10g dietary fiber

(continued on page 65)

Chia Breakfast Custard
(continued from page 64)

Now pour the cream-yolk mixture into your chia seeds and stir the whole thing up with your fork, again breaking up any clumps. Make sure you stir all the way down to the bottom of the bowl so that you catch any clumps of unincorporated chia seeds and mix them in.

Put your chia custard in the microwave and give it 1 minute on Medium (50 percent). Stir it, give it 1 more minute, again on Medium, and it's done!

Yield: 1 serving

Coconut "Corn Flakes"
I confess to finding this idea online, on the Satisfying Eats Web site; this is my adaptation of Melissa Monroe McGehee's idea. It's really good and remarkably cereal-like. Note that this needs the larger flaked coconut, not the shredded finer variety. Eat as you would corn flakes: Add a little cream or half-and-half and a sprinkle of Swerve or Splenda (or some more liquid stevia) and dig in.

4 cups (320 g) flaked coconut

½ teaspoon salt

¼ teaspoon liquid stevia— (English toffee flavor)

1 teaspoon vanilla extract

¼ cup (60 ml) water

¼ cup (60 g) powdered Swerve

Per serving: 143 calories; 13g fat (79.9% calories from fat); 1g protein; 6g carbohydrate; 4g dietary fiber

Preheat the oven to 325°F (170°C, or gas mark 3). Line a large shallow baking pan with aluminum foil.

Place the coconut flakes in a large bowl. Stir the salt, stevia, and vanilla extract into the water, stirring until the salt is dissolved.

A tablespoon (15 ml) at a time, sprinkle the seasoned water over the coconut, mixing very thoroughly after each addition. You want to wind up with all the coconut flakes evenly coated with the seasoning mixture. Now, again, 1 tablespoon (15 g) at a time, add the Swerve, stirring after each addition, till all the coconut is evenly coated.

Spread the coconut in an even layer in the prepared baking pan. Bake for 15 minutes, then stir everything carefully but well, and spread it out evenly again. Continue baking, stirring every 5 minutes, until the flakes are evenly golden; this should take another 10 to 15 minutes. Don't neglect to stir every 5 minutes! The oven timer is your friend here.

Let cool and store in a snap-top container.

Yield: 8 servings

Quiche Crust

Often, low-carbers just skip the crust when making quiche, but I like the texture contrast the crust provides.

1 cup (145 g) raw sunflower seed kernels

1½ cups (168 g) almond meal

½ cup (50 g) grated Parmesan cheese

¼ cup (56 g) coconut oil

½ teaspoon xanthan, guar, or glucomannan

½ teaspoon salt

1 tablespoon (15 ml) water

Per serving: 193 calories; 15g fat (64.3% calories from fat); 11g protein; 7g carbohydrate; 1g dietary fiber

Preheat the oven to 350°F (180°C, or gas mark 4). Grease a 10-inch (25.5 cm) pie plate or coat with nonstick cooking spray.

Put the sunflower seeds in your food processor and run it till they're a fine meal. Add the almond meal, Parmesan, coconut oil, xanthan, and salt and pulse till it's all well blended. Then, with the processor running, add the water. The dough should form a cohesive glob.

Turn off the processor and turn the dough out into the prepared pie plate. Use clean hands to pat it out evenly, all over the bottom and up the sides of the pie plate.

Bake for 12 minutes or until it is starting to color with a touch of gold. Let it cool while you prepare whatever quiche filling you are using.

Yield: 12 servings

Crackers

The crackers included here are crunchy, flavorful, and all-around cracker-y. However, they are not up to the 70 percent calories from fat standard. Why, then, did I include them? First, one of the things people long for on low-carb diets is crunchy, salty stuff. And anyway, crackers are often paired with something fattier: a dip, a spread, cheese, something like that. So, make some crackers!

TWO NOTES:

1) Do not, do not, *do not* skip the baking parchment. No matter how much grease or cooking spray you use, you will regret it. Learn from my mistakes.

2) If you find yourself making crackers often—and you may—get yourself down to the local housewares store, or onto the ever-popular Amazon.com, and buy a set of silicone rings for your rolling pin. These look sort of like pairs of rubber bands in various thicknesses; you put one around either end of your rolling pin and they let you roll things out perfectly evenly, as thin as you please. I use the thinnest in my set of rings for all of these crackers.

Rich and Tender Crackers

The name says it all: These versatile crackers have a tender, buttery crunch.

1 cup (145 g) raw sunflower seed kernals

½ cup (65 g) rice protein powder

2 teaspoons xanthan

½ teaspoon baking powder

½ teaspoon salt, plus more for sprinkling

4 tablespoons (55 g) butter, softened

1 egg white

1 tablespoon (15 ml) water

Per serving: 34 calories; 2g fat (61.4% calories from fat); 3g protein; 1g carbohydrate; trace dietary fiber

Preheat the oven to 350°F (180°C, or gas mark 4).

Put the sunflower seeds, rice protein powder, xanthan, baking powder, and salt in your food processor, and run it till the whole thing is a fine, even meal.

Add the butter and run the processor until it's well incorporated. Add the egg white and again run till it's incorporated. Finally, add the water and run till you have a soft dough.

Line a cookie sheet with baking parchment. Make a ball of half the dough and place in the middle of the parchment. Cover with another sheet of parchment and with a rolling pin, roll out into as thin and even a sheet as you can. Peel off the top sheet of parchment. Using a thin, sharp, straight-bladed knife, score the dough into squares, diamonds, or triangles; I make mine about the size of Wheat Thins.

Bake for 25 minutes or until golden. While they're baking, roll out and cut the rest of the dough on a second cookie sheet. When the first batch is done, bake the second.

Cool on the cookie sheets, re-score to break apart, and store in a snap-top container.

Yield: 50 servings

Rosemary-Cheese Crackers

I saw a recipe somewhere for rosemary-cheese crackers, and while I wasn't going to use flour and all that stuff, the flavor combination sounded great. It is! These may be the best crackers I've ever done.

1 cup (145 g) sunflower seed kernals

½ cup (65 g) rice protein powder

½ teaspoon xanthan or guar

½ teaspoon baking powder

½ teaspoon salt, plus more for sprinkling

2 tablespoons (28 g) butter, softened

1½ tablespoons (3 g) minced fresh rosemary

1 cup (115 g) shredded sharp Cheddar cheese

½ cup (50 g) shredded Parmesan cheese

1 egg white

3 tablespoons (45 ml) water

Per cracker: 42 calories; 3g fat (60.3% calories from fat); 3g protein; 1g carbohydrate; trace dietary fiber

Preheat the oven to 350°F (180°C, or gas mark 4).

Put the sunflower seeds, rice protein powder, xanthan or guar, baking powder, and salt in your food processor and run it till the sunflower seeds are ground up to the texture of cornmeal or finer.

With the processor running, add the butter and the rosemary. Then work in the cheeses in three or four additions.

With the processor still running, add the egg white, then the water. When you have a soft dough, turn off the processor.

Line a cookie sheet with baking parchment. Make a ball of half the dough, put it on the parchment, and then put another sheet of parchment over it. Use your rolling pin to roll the dough out into as thin and even a sheet as you can. Carefully peel off the top sheet of parchment. Using a thin, sharp, straight-bladed knife, score the dough into crackers; I make mine about the size of Wheat Thins. Sprinkle them lightly with salt.

Bake for 20 to 25 minutes or until golden. While they're baking, roll out and cut the rest of the dough on a second cookie sheet. When the first batch is done, bake the second.

Cool on the cookie sheets, re-score to break apart, and store in a snap-top container.

Yield: About 50 crackers

Anchovy-Olive Crackers

Inspiration for these crackers started with a recipe I saw in a Spanish cookbook. I wasn't going to use wheat flour, of course, but the flavor combination seemed interesting and was well worth adapting.

1½ cups (218 g) sunflower seed kernals

½ teaspoon baking powder

½ teaspoon xanthan or guar

½ cup (50 g) grated Parmesan or romano cheese, or a combination of the two

8 anchovy fillets packed in olive oil

3 tablespoons (19 g) chopped black olives

1 tablespoon (15 ml) water

Salt

Per cracker: 30 calories; 3g fat (70.2% calories from fat); 2g protein; 1g carbohydrate; trace dietary fiber

Preheat the oven to 350°F (180°C, or gas mark 4).

Put the sunflower seeds, baking powder, and xanthan or guar in your food processor and run it until the seeds are a fine meal.

Add the Parmesan and anchovy fillets and run the processor until the anchovies are pulverized and completely incorporated.

Add the chopped olives and the water. Pulse just enough to combine; you want flecks of olive to be visible in the finished crackers.

Line a cookie sheet with baking parchment. Make a ball of half the dough and place in the middle of the parchment. Cover with another sheet of parchment and using a rolling pin, roll into as thin and even a sheet as you can. Peel off the top parchment, sprinkle the dough with salt, and then use a sharp, thin, straight-bladed knife to score into squares, diamonds, or triangles; I make mine about the size of Wheat Thins.

Bake for 25 minutes or until golden. While they're baking, roll out and cut the rest of the dough on a second cookie sheet. When the first batch is done, bake the second.

Cool on the cookie sheet, re-score to break apart and store in a snap-top container.

Yield: About 50 crackers

Eggs

How much do I love eggs? I love eggs fried, scrambled, poached, boiled, in omelets, in quiches—just about any way you can imagine. (Except raw. My husband will occasionally crack a couple of eggs into a glass and swig them down for a quick protein hit. Not me.) I love eggs so much I have 20-odd chickens in my backyard.

Add to this that eggs are endlessly versatile, consistently affordable (around here, even the good local pastured eggs run $3 to $3.50 per dozen), keep well in the fridge, and can be cooked in a flash, and it's easy to see why, when I'm not sure what to cook, my instinct is to reach for the eggs.

Don't be fooled by the term *free-range*. This means very little—just that the chickens have a small door they could go through to get out to a fenced-in run of some kind, but probably don't. Pastured eggs, on the other hand, come from chickens allowed to run around eating grass and bugs and anything else that gets in their way. (Do not believe the popular mythology that chickens are vegetarians. They're little dinosaurs, and heaven help the bug or lizard or salamander or baby snake who crosses their paths. My chickens will eat almost anything, but they fight over meat scraps. And if you're considering backyard chickens, I will give you this encouragement: They turn ticks into food. That has to be the neatest magic trick around. They're also really funny.)

Please, please, do not throw away egg yolks. If you're reading this book, you're less likely than the general population to be yolk-o-phobic, but just in case, let me be clear: Nearly all the vitamins and antioxidants in an egg are in the yolk. You'd do better to throw away the whites, though I don't recommend that, either. Just figure eggs are perfect the way they come out of the bird and treat them with the love and respect they deserve.

Creamy Scrambled Eggs
Here's the classical method of scrambling eggs, resulting in a creamy, almost custardlike texture.

1 tablespoon (14 g) butter

3 large eggs

1 tablespoon (15 ml) heavy cream

¼ teaspoon salt

⅛ teaspoon ground black pepper

1 tablespoon (3 g) chopped fresh chives or (6 g) minced scallion (optional)

Per serving: 351 calories; 30g fat (77.9% calories from fat); 17g protein; 2g carbohydrate; trace dietary fiber

Heat a medium-size skillet, preferably nonstick, over low heat. Throw in the butter and let it melt while you break the eggs into a dish and scramble them up.

When the butter is all melted, slosh it around to cover the whole bottom of the skillet and then pour in the eggs. Unlike the usual methods, the pan should not be hot enough to make the eggs sizzle when they hit.

Let the eggs sit until they're starting to set on the bottom, maybe 30 seconds. Then scramble, keeping the heat low and the curds fine

When the eggs are about two-thirds set, add the cream, salt and pepper, and the chives, if using. Continue scrambling for another 30 to 60 seconds until the cream is blended in and then serve.

Yield: 1 serving

Dana's Easy Omelet Method

This section will appear oddly familiar to those of you who have read my other books. That's because I have repeated these instructions in most of them and will continue to do so until the entire population of the world knows how to turn out a perfect omelet in 5 minutes flat.

If I had to choose just one skill to teach to everyone trying to improve his or her diet, it would be how to make an omelet. They're fast, they're easy, and they turn a wide variety of simple ingredients into a meal!

First, have your filling ready. If you're using vegetables, you'll want to sauté them first. If you're making an omelet to use up leftovers (a great idea, by the way), warm them in the microwave and have them standing by. If you're using cheese, either grate it beforehand or have the grater and block of cheese standing by.

The pan matters. For omelets, I recommend an 8- to 9-inch (20 to 23 cm) nonstick skillet with sloping sides. Put it over medium-high heat. While the skillet's heating, grab your eggs—two is the perfect number for this size pan, but one or three will work—and a bowl, crack the eggs, and beat them with a fork. Don't add anything, just mix them up.

The pan is hot enough when a drop of water thrown in sizzles right away. Add a little fat, whatever works with the ingredients of your omelet, and slosh it around to cover the bottom. Now pour in the eggs, all at once. They should sizzle and immediately start to set. When the bottom layer of egg is set around the edges—this should happen quite quickly —lift the edge using a spatula or fork and tip the pan to let the raw egg flow underneath. Do this all around the edges until there's not enough raw egg to run.

Next, turn your burner to the lowest heat if you have a gas stove. If you have an electric stove, you'll have to have a "warm" burner standing by; electric elements don't cool off fast enough for this job. Put your filling on one half of the omelet, cover it, and let it sit over very low heat for a minute or two, no more. Peek and see if the raw, shiny egg on the top surface has cooked. (Although you can serve it that way if you like. That's how the French prefer their omelets.) If you're using cheese, you'll want to check that it's melted, too.

When your omelet is done, slip a spatula under the half without the filling, fold it over the filling, and then lift the whole thing onto a plate.

This makes a single-serving omelet. I think it's a lot easier to make several individual omelets than to make one big one, and omelets are so fast to make that it's not that big a deal. And that way you can customize your omelets to each individual's taste. If you're making more than two or three omelets, just keep them warm in your oven, set to its very lowest heat.

Now for some things to put in your omelets! I am famous for wrapping any and everything in an eggy envelope. Start looking at foods, especially bits of leftovers, with omelet potential in mind!

Buttery Mushroom and Swiss Omelet

This is pure cheesy, buttery, mushroom-y goodness! If you want to be fancy, you could use Havarti instead. But good ol' Swiss is delicious.

1 tablespoon (10 g) minced onion
2 ounces (55 g) mushrooms, sliced
2 tablespoons (28 g) butter, divided
Pinch of ground nutmeg
2 large eggs
1½ ounces (43 g) Swiss cheese, sliced or shredded

Per serving: 513 calories; 44g fat (76.2% calories from fat); 25g protein; 6g carbohydrate; 1g dietary fiber

Mince the onion and slice the mushrooms, if you didn't buy 'em that way.

Put your omelet skillet over medium heat, melt 1½ tablespoons (21 g) of the butter, and sauté the onion and mushrooms with the nutmeg until the onion is translucent and the mushrooms have softened. Transfer to a plate.

Give the pan a quick wipe, if you think it needs it, and then put it back over the burner and turn the heat up to medium-high. While it's heating, scramble up the eggs.

When the pan is hot, melt the remaining butter and make your omelet according to Dana's Easy Omelet Method on page 72. Put the Swiss cheese in first, topped with the mushroom mixture. Cover, turn the burner to low, and let it cook till the cheese is melted. Fold and serve.

Yield: 1 serving

Jalapeño–Cream Cheese Omelet

Here is yet another simple combination that comes out incredibly well. If you mix up a double or triple batch of the filling and stash it in the fridge, there's breakfast or supper for a few days.

1 tablespoon (9 g) chopped jarred jalapeño pepper
2 teaspoons minced fresh cilantro
1 scallion, thinly sliced
1½ ounces (43 g) cream cheese
2 teaspoons bacon grease
2 large eggs

*Per serving: 365 calories; 32g fat (**80.1% calories from fat**); 15g protein; 4g carbohydrate; 1g dietary fiber*

This is pretty darned easy: Put the jalapeño, cilantro, scallion, and cream cheese in your food processor and pulse until the everything's chopped together. Or you can just chop the jalapeño, cilantro, and scallion and work them into the cream cheese with the back of a fork.

Using the bacon grease and eggs, make your omelet using Dana's Easy Omelet Method on page 72, with the cream cheese mixture as the filling, and then yum it down!

Yield: 1 serving

Liverwurst Omelet

I love liverwurst, surely a harmless quirk. Back when I was a carbivore, I loved liverwurst, tomato, and alfalfa sprout sandwiches made with whole wheat bagels, and that combo gave me the idea for this omelet. Because of the liver, this is particularly high in vitamins.

1 tablespoon (14 g) butter or bacon grease

2 large eggs

2 ounces (55 g) liverwurst, sliced

½ a medium tomato, sliced

1 tablespoon (14 g) mayonnaise

1 tablespoon (5 g) grated Parmesan cheese

Using the butter and eggs, make your omelet according to Dana's Easy Omelet Method on page 72. Fill with the liverwurst first and then add the sliced tomato on top.

Fold the omelet, top with the mayonnaise and Parmesan, and serve.

Yield: 1 serving

Per serving: 552 calories; 50g fat ***(80.5% calories from fat)***; *22g protein; 5g carbohydrate; 1g dietary fiber*

Mushroom-Bacon Omelet

This is what I did with my Hongos Chipotles the day I first made them. This is also good with shredded Monterey Jack cheese added. If you use the cheese, layer it in first, with the mushroom mixture and bacon on top.

¼ of a batch Hongos Chipotles (page 101)

3 bacon slices

2 teaspoons coconut oil

2 large eggs

If the Hongos Chipotles have been in the refrigerator, warm them through before making the omelet.

Cook the bacon—me, I'd nuke it for about 5 minutes on High, but do as you will.

Using the coconut oil and eggs, make your omelet according to Dana's Easy Omelet Method on page 72, layering in the mushroom mixture. Add the bacon right before folding. Serve!

Yield: 1 serving

Per serving: 421 calories; 38g fat (79.9% calories from fat); 18g protein; 4g carbohydrate; 1g dietary fiber

Spinach-Artichoke Omelet

When I was creating the Artichoke-Spinach Dip/Filling on page 38, I was thinking of stuffing it into mushrooms, which I did. While I was stuffing the mushrooms, I thought "Omelet!" You could add sautéed mushrooms to this omelet to good effect, but the dip makes for an excellent omelet all on its own.

2 teaspoons coconut oil

2 large eggs

⅓ cup (77 g) Artichoke-Spinach Dip/Filling

This is simplicity itself: Make your omelet according to Dana's Easy Omelet Method on page 72, filling it with the Artichoke-Spinach Dip/Filling.

Yield: 1 serving

Per serving: 483 calories; 43g fat (77.9% calories from fat); 20g protein; 7g carbohydrate; 1g dietary fiber

Chipotle Chicken and Avocado Omelet

With leftover rotisserie chicken and leftover Chipotle Mayonnaise, I could have made a salad, but an omelet sounded so much better. If you don't have Chipotle Mayonnaise in the fridge, you can spike regular mayo with Tabasco Chipotle, a little lime juice, and a pinch or two of cumin—it's not the same, but still good.

¼ cup (35 g) diced cooked chicken

2 teaspoons minced red onion

2 teaspoons minced fresh cilantro

1½ tablespoons (20 g) Chipotle Mayonnaise (page 45)

2 teaspoons coconut oil

2 large eggs

1 ounce (28 g) jalapeño Jack cheese, shredded

½ an avocado

Put the chicken, red onion, and cilantro in a bowl. Add the Chipotle Mayonnaise and mix it all up.

Now, using the coconut oil and eggs, make your omelet according to Dana's Easy Omelet Method on page 72. Put the cheese in first and then spread the chicken mixture over that. Turn the burner to low, cover the skillet, and let it cook while you peel and slice your avocado half. Take the lid off the skillet long enough to arrange the avocado slices over the other ingredients. Re-cover until the cheese is melted and the chicken is warm.

Fold and serve!

Yield: 1 very filling serving

Per serving: 800 calories; 72g fat (79.4% calories from fat); 32g protein; 11g carbohydrate; 3g dietary fiber

Sausage, Pepper, and Avocado Omelet

My instincts run toward cheese in omelets, but I know a lot of folks are dairy-free. This is as good and as filling as any omelet with cheese—you won't be hungry for hours and hours.

2 ounces (55 g) pork sausage

¼ cup (38 g) diced red bell pepper

¼ cup (40 g) diced onion

½ cup (40 g) chopped mushrooms

1 tablespoon (14 g) bacon grease

Salt and ground black pepper

1 tablespoon (14 g) coconut oil

2 large eggs

½ an avocado, peeled and sliced

Per serving: 799 calories; 74g fat (81.6% calories from fat); 21g protein; 17g carbohydrate; 4g dietary fiber

Put your omelet skillet over medium heat and start browning and crumbling the sausage. Add the bell pepper, onion, and mushrooms to the sausage, along with the bacon grease. Sauté everything till the sausage is done, the onions are translucent, and the mushrooms have softened. Scoop this all out onto a plate and reserve.

Wipe your pan to remove any sticky residue. Put it back over the burner and turn it up to medium-high.

Melt the coconut oil and make your omelet according to Dana's Easy Omelet Method on page 72, layering in the sausage mixture first, then the avocado slices on top.

When it's done, fold and eat! You may want to share this with a friend. It really is that filling.

Yield: 1 serving

Creamy Parmesan Eggs

This is a nice breakfast to serve when you have guests staying over: It's easy, kind of fancy, and everybody's eggs cook at once.

8 large eggs

6 tablespoons (90 ml) heavy cream

¼ cup (25 g) grated Parmesan cheese

2 teaspoons butter

Per serving: 248 calories; 20g fat (75% calories from fat); 14g protein; 2g carbohydrate; 0g dietary fiber

Preheat the oven to 325°F (170°C, or gas mark 3). Grease 4 ramekins, or coat with nonstick cooking spray.

Break 2 eggs into each ramekin. Float 1½ tablespoons (23 ml) of heavy cream on each and then scatter 1 tablespoon (5 g) of Parmesan over each. Dot each with ½ teaspoon of butter.

Put the ramekins in the oven and bake for 12 to 18 minutes, depending on how done each person likes his or her eggs (17 minutes is about right for me).

Serve hot!

Yield: 4 servings

Avocado Baked Eggs

This is a new favorite! The cheese is not essential here, but trust me, you will like it. I usually can eat three eggs, but with half an avocado, I was satisfied with just one—well, one egg and some extra bacon.

2 bacon slices

1 avocado, just ripe but not squishy

½ teaspoon Creole seasoning

2 large eggs

2 ounces (55 g) Monterey Jack cheese, shredded or sliced (optional)

Per serving: 372 calories; 32g fat (73.8% calories from fat); 16g protein; 9g carbohydrate; 3g dietary fiber

Preheat the oven to 400°F (200°C, or gas mark 6).

First cook the bacon, however you like to cook it, until it's crisp.

Halve the avocado and remove the pit. Use the tip of a spoon to scoop out a little more flesh from the cavity, so that it's big enough to hold an egg. Reserve the flesh you remove for a salad, or just eat it.

Use a sharp, thin-bladed knife to score the flesh in a crisscross pattern, making squares about ½-inch (1.3 cm).

Spray 2 ramekins that will accomodate an avocado with nonstick cooking spray or grease them well. Fit an avocado half down into each—my ramekins were just big enough to each hold an avocado half.

Spoon a little of the bacon grease into each avocado half and spread it so it gets down into the scoring. Sprinkle each with the Creole seasoning.

Break an egg into each avocado half. Put the ramekins in the oven and set a timer for 12 minutes.

When it beeps, check and see how done your eggs look; the timing will depend on the size of both your eggs and avocados. If they're still underdone, give them another few minutes.

If you're using the cheese, cover each egg with half of it about 2 minutes before removing the ramekins from the oven.

When the eggs are done to your liking, remove from the oven, putting them on something heatproof! Snip or crumble a slice of bacon over each and serve from the ramekins.

Yield: 2 servings

Creamy Asparagus Frittata

Great for Sunday brunch or an easy one-pan supper, this frittata reheats beautifully in the microwave, too, so making this over the weekend could potentially give you quick breakfasts all week long.

4 tablespoons (55 g) butter

½ a small onion

1 pound (455 g) asparagus (Slender stalks are best for this.)

8 large eggs

1 cup (110 g) shredded Swiss cheese

½ cup (50 g) grated Parmesan cheese, divided

½ cup (120 ml) dry white wine

¼ cup (60 ml) heavy cream

½ teaspoon dried thyme

½ teaspoon salt or Vege-Sal, or 1 teaspoon Beautiful World Seasoning (page 51)

Per serving: 238 calories; 18g fat (72% calories from fat); 13g protein; 4g carbohydrate; 1g dietary fiber

Coat your large, heavy oven-safe skillet with nonstick cooking spray and put it over medium-low heat. Melt the butter and start sautéing the onion.

Snap the ends off the asparagus where they want to break naturally. Lay the stalks on a cutting board and cut into ½ inch (1.3 cm) lengths.

In a bowl, whisk together all of the remaining ingredients.

When the onion is soft, add the asparagus to the skillet and sauté it for a minute or two, just till it turns brighter green.

Add the egg mixture to the skillet and stir it around so the onion and asparagus are evenly distributed. Now turn the burner to low, cover the skillet, and cook for 15 to 20 minutes. (Set a timer!)

Check your frittata. If the top is still really runny, give it another 5 to 10 minutes. When the top is just a little runny, you're ready for the last step.

Turn on the broiler and slide the skillet into the oven, about 6 inches (15 cm) from the heat. Broil till the top is just touched with gold. Cut into wedges and serve.

Yield: 8 servings

Eggs al Diavolo
If your fridge and pantry look anything like mine, this is a great one-dish meal that can be made with stuff that you already have on hand.

¼ cup (60 ml) olive oil

½ a medium onion, thinly sliced

2 cloves garlic, crushed

1 can (14 ounces, or 390 g) diced tomatoes

½ cup (50 g) sliced green olives

2 tablespoons (30 g) pesto sauce, homemade (see page 45) or purchased

¼ teaspoon red pepper flakes

6 large eggs

½ cup (60 g) shredded mozzarella cheese

3 tablespoons (15 g) grated Parmesan cheese

Per serving: 495 calories; 40g fat (72.1% calories from fat); 20g protein; 15g carbohydrate; 1g dietary fiber

In your large, heavy skillet over medium heat, warm the olive oil and sauté the onion until translucent. Stir in the garlic.

Add the canned tomatoes, juice and all, the olives, pesto, and red pepper flakes. Stir everything up.

Use the back of your mixing spoon to make a hollow in the vegetable mixture and break an egg into it. Repeat until all the eggs are in. Cover the skillet and turn the heat to low.

Check after about 5 minutes to see how well done your eggs are. You're shooting for the whites being set but the yolks still runny.

When the eggs are almost to the point you want, scatter the mozzarella evenly over everything. Let it melt and then transfer to serving plates. Scatter a tablespoon (5 g) of Parmesan over each serving and serve.

Yield: 3 servings

Eggs in Avocado Frames
I loved "eggs in a frame" as a kid. Once I'd made the Hot, Crunchy Avocado on page 107, and noticed the nice hole in the middle of the biggest slices, this became inevitable.

1 avocado

3 large eggs

2 teaspoons water

½ cup (60 g) pork rind crumbs

1 tablespoon (7 g) coconut flour

⅓ cup (75 g) coconut oil

Per serving: 667 calories; 61g fat (79.7% calories from fat); 24g protein; 11g carbohydrate; 5g dietary fiber

Cut the avocado in half, remove the pit, and cut a ½-inch-thick (1.3 cm) slice from either side. Reserve the rest of the avocado for a salad or guacamole later in the day. Peel your 2 slices with the nice, big holes in the middle.

On a rimmed plate, beat one of the eggs with the water. Spread the Pork Rind Crumbs on another plate.

Dust both sides of the avocado slices with the coconut flour, then dip in the egg wash, and then in the pork rind crumbs, making a thick coating.

(continued on page 80)

Eggs in Avocado Frames
(continued from page 79)

Let your "breaded" avocado sit while you heat your large, heavy skillet over medium heat. If it's not nonstick, you might give it a squirt of cooking spray. Melt the coconut oil and then add the avocado slices. Fry them until nice and brown and crunchy on the bottom, then flip.

When you flip the avocado slices, break each of the remaining eggs into the hole in the center of one of the avocado slices. Cover the skillet and let them cook for a few minutes.

Uncover the skillet, flip the egg-filled avocado slices carefully, and let them cook just for another minute, to set the whites. Serve.

Yield: 2 servings

Breakfast Casserole
This is a great way to serve breakfast for a crowd. It reheats well, too, so if you make it over the weekend, you've got breakfast for several days.

16 bacon slices, diced

½ a medium onion, diced

8 large eggs

2 cups (225 g) shredded Cheddar cheese, divided

1½ cups (165 g) shredded Swiss cheese, divided

1 cup (225 g) full-fat creamed cottage cheese

½ cup (120 ml) heavy cream

¾ teaspoon salt

¼ teaspoon ground black pepper

4 cups (400 g) diced cauliflower

Per serving: 426 calories; 33g fat (68.9% calories from fat); 27g protein; 6g carbohydrate; 1g dietary fiber

Preheat the oven to 350°F (180°C, or gas mark 4). Grease a 3-quart (2.8 L) casserole or coat with nonstick cooking spray.

In your large skillet over medium-low heat, cook the bacon till the bits are crispy. Scoop out of the skillet with a slotted spoon and reserve on a plate.

Cook the onion in the bacon grease in the skillet till it's translucent.

Whisk the eggs with half the Cheddar, half the Swiss, the cottage cheese, and cream. Stir in half the bacon bits and the salt and pepper. Mix the cauliflower into it all and spoon it into the casserole.

Top with the remaining Cheddar, Swiss, and bacon bits. Bake for 45 minutes and serve hot.

Yield: 8 servings

Chicken-Pecan Quiche

Oh, man, this is good. If you make it ahead, it reheats beautifully by the slice in the microwave and is great any time of day.

1 cup (25 g) pecans

2 tablespoons (28 g) bacon grease

1 large shallot, minced

6 ounces (170 g) Swiss cheese, shredded

1 prepared Quiche Crust (page 60)

1 cup (140 g) diced cooked chicken

5 large eggs

1 cup (235 ml) heavy cream

2 tablespoons (28 ml) dry white wine

1 teaspoon seasoned salt (or you could use a couple of teaspoons of the Beautiful World Seasoning on page 51)

1 teaspoon paprika

4 dashes of hot pepper sauce

¼ teaspoon ground black pepper

Per serving: 577 calories; 46g fat (69.5% calories from fat); 32g protein; 13g carbohydrate; 2g dietary fiber

Preheat the oven to 325°F (170°C, or gas mark 3). Spread the pecans on a shallow baking pan and put them in the oven. Set your timer for 7 minutes.

In a small skillet over medium heat, melt the bacon grease and sauté the shallot until it's soft and golden. Remove from the heat.

By now the pecans are toasted. Pull 'em out of the oven!

Spread the Swiss cheese in an even layer in the bottom of the Quiche Crust. Spread the chicken evenly over the cheese. Spread the pecans on top of the chicken. Your finished quiche will be prettiest if you turn them all convex side up, but it's hardly essential.

Now using a whisk or your blender, combine all the remaining ingredients. Pour over the filling.

Bake until set, about 1 hour, but check it at 50 minutes. You want it set through, but not overbaked.

Yield: 8 servings

Eggs with Peppers and Onions

The first time I tried this out, I actually made a half-recipe, and it worked out nicely. If you want to do that, just use a smaller skillet.

6 bacon slices

¼ cup (60 ml) olive oil

½ cup (75 g) thinly sliced green bell pepper

½ cup (80 g) thinly sliced onion

2 cloves of garlic, crushed

2 teaspoons paprika (I use Hungarian, but whatever you have should be fine.)

1 teaspoon Creole seasoning

8 large eggs

Per serving: 326 calories; 27g fat (75.1% calories from fat); 15g protein; 6g carbohydrate; 1g dietary fiber

First, put your big skillet over medium-low heat and fry the bacon until crisp. Transfer it to a plate and reserve.

If it looks like you have more than 4 tablespoons (60 ml) of bacon grease in the skillet, pour off a little into your bacon grease jar. (You have a bacon grease jar, right?) Put the pan back on the burner.

Add the olive oil to the bacon grease and turn up the heat to medium. Add the bell pepper and onion and sauté till the onion is just turning translucent. Crush in the garlic, paprika, and Creole seasoning. Stir it up.

With the back of a spoon, make 8 hollows in the vegetable mixture and break an egg into each.

Turn the burner to low and cover the pan. Set a timer for 5 minutes. Check and if the eggs are still underdone, give them a few more minutes—you want the whites set but the yolks still runny.

Transfer to serving plates, crumble the bacon over the top, and serve.

Yield: 4 servings

Side Salads and Dressings

CHAPTER 5

I **realize that this chapter** is missing simple green salads—you know, the lettuce-y sort of thing. So I will say a few words on the subject: All lettuces and other leafy greens are very low in both carbs and calories. Iceberg, romaine, butter lettuce, red leaf, radicchio, chicory, spinach, arugula; whatever you choose, if you toss it with an oil-based dressing, you can pretty much count on the results being very low-carb, with a high fat percentage. Adding other very low-carb vegetables won't mess this up, of course. These include but are not limited to: alfalfa sprouts, broccoli (and broccoli sprouts), cabbage, cauliflower, celery, cucumbers, peppers, radishes, mushrooms, parsley, and zucchini and other summer squashes. Tomatoes, onions, and carrots are a little higher in carbs, but you'd have to eat a lot of them to really spike your blood sugar.

Just eat your salad with a high-fat dressing, and you'll be fine.

Throw in some crumbled bacon, toasted nuts, maybe some feta or blue cheese, what the heck—it's all good.

The dressings are at the end of this chapter, but I often don't bother mixing up a dressing. Instead, I crush a clove of garlic into a custard cup and cover it with extra-virgin olive oil. I assemble my salad, pour on the oil, and toss till everything is coated. Then I sprinkle on some vinegar—wine vinegar, balsamic, whatever seems to fit—and toss again. If I want a creamy dressing, I'll throw in a dollop of mayonnaise. Maybe add a squirt of mustard, or a sprinkle of herbs or Parmesan, and again, toss like mad; then finally add salt and pepper. It's easy.

Asparagus-Strawberry Salad

Tester Burma rates this a perfect 10 and says, "It's one of those dishes that would evoke a 'wow' because it's so pretty, and it tastes as good as it looks. The results belie the lack of time and effort required."

1 pound (455 g) asparagus

2 cups (290 g) strawberries

1 batch Another Poppy Seed Dressing (page 93)

12 lettuce leaves (I'd go with butter lettuce.)

¼ cup (30 g) crumbled blue cheese

Per serving: 136 calories; 12g fat (73.8% calories from fat); 3g protein; 7g carbohydrate; 2g dietary fiber

Snap the ends off the asparagus where they want to break naturally. Lay the spears on your cutting board and cut it into 1-inch (2.5 cm) lengths. Put 'em in a microwaveable casserole with a lid or a microwave steamer, add a couple of tablespoons (28 ml) water, cover, and nuke on High for 3 minutes—you want it tender-crisp and brilliantly green. When the asparagus is done, uncover it immediately to stop the cooking, drain it, and put it in an ice water bath; then drain and put it in the fridge. Let it chill for at least 1 hour.

Remove the hulls from the strawberries and quarter them. Put the asparagus and strawberries in your salad bowl. Give the Another Poppy Seed Dressing a good shake, pour it over the asparagus and strawberries, and toss.

Line 6 plates with the lettuce. Toss the asparagus and strawberries again and then pile on top of the lettuce. Top each serving with blue cheese and serve.

Yield: 6 servings

Brooklyn Deli Unpotato Salad
The recipe I adapted this from claimed that this is what you'd find in a Brooklyn Jewish deli—except for the fact that it doesn't actually contain potatoes, of course. You can buy your green olives already sliced, which is a good idea.

1 head of cauliflower (Trim the very bottom stem.)

3 celery ribs, diced

¼ of a large red onion, diced

¾ cup (75 g) sliced green olives with pimientos

⅓ cup (20 g) chopped fresh parsley

¼ cup (60 ml) extra-virgin olive oil

¼ cup (60 ml) wine vinegar

2 tablespoons (30 g) brown mustard

½ teaspoon celery seeds

¾ cup (175 g) mayonnaise

Salt and ground black pepper

3 hard-boiled eggs

*Per serving: 276 calories; 30g fat **(92.7% calories from fat)**; 3g protein; 2g carbohydrate; trace dietary fiber*

Cut the entire cauliflower into ½-inch (1.3 cm) chunks. Put them in a microwaveable casserole with a lid, or a microwave steamer, add a couple of tablespoons (28 ml) of water, cover, and nuke on High for 10 minutes—you want the cauliflower tender but not mushy.

Drain the cauliflower well and put it in a big bowl. Add the celery, onion, olives, and parsley.

Put the olive oil, vinegar, mustard, celery seeds, and mayonnaise in your blender and run till it's smooth and well combined. Pour the dressing over the salad and stir to coat. Season with salt and pepper to taste.

Finally, peel the hard-boiled eggs, halve them, lay the halves face down on your chopping board, and dice. Add to the salad and stir gently so as to maintain some hunks of yolk. Chill before serving.

Yield: 8 servings

Sprightly Spinach Salad
Burma loved this colorful salad as is, but she suggests you should try it with a vinaigrette sometime, too. Burma is an excellent cook, so trust her!

4 bacon slices

1 navel orange

6 cups (180 g) baby spinach

½ cup (35 g) shredded red cabbage

½ cup (35 g) sliced mushrooms

⅛ of a red onion, sliced paper-thin

½ a batch Bacon-Roasted Garlic Ranch Dressing (page 92)

*Per serving: 139 calories; 13g fat **(81.9% calories from fat)**; 3g protein; 3g carbohydrate; 1g dietary fiber*

Start the bacon cooking—I'd probably microwave mine on High for 6 minutes, but follow your preference. Just get it crisp.

Peel the orange, picking off all the white bits you can. Separate the sections and then cut each section into ½-inch (1.3 cm) lengths.

Pile the spinach onto 6 plates. Top each serving with red cabbage, then mushrooms, onion, and orange bits.

Drizzle 2 tablespoons (30 g) of Bacon-Roasted Garlic Ranch Dressing over each salad. Crumble up the bacon, divide it between the salads, and serve immediately.

Yield: 6 servings

Barbecue Salad

This started as a macaroni salad, but I fixed that with the versatile cauliflower. It's creamy, savory, luscious, and perfect with any grilled or smoked meat! This is best made at least a few hours in advance; put it in the fridge and let the flavors all get friendly.

½ a head of cauliflower (Trim the very bottom stem.)

1 bunch scallions, sliced

½ cup (75 g) diced bell pepper, diced (I used a mix of red, orange, and yellow, but use whatever sweet bell pepper you have.)

½ cup (60 g) diced celery

¾ cup (175 g) mayonnaise

¼ cup (60 g) sour cream

2 teaspoons soy sauce

1 clove of garlic, crushed

1 teaspoon dry mustard

½ teaspoon paprika

½ teaspoon onion powder

½ teaspoon ground black pepper

⅛ teaspoon cayenne pepper

Salt

Cut the cauliflower into ½-inch (1.3 cm) chunks. Put them in a microwaveable casserole dish with a lid or a microwave steamer and nuke on High for 10 to 12 minutes. You want it tender but not mushy.

Meanwhile, put the scallions, bell pepper, and celery in a large bowl. Stir together the mayonnaise, sour cream, soy sauce, garlic, dry mustard, paprika, onion powder, black pepper, and cayenne. You will be unsurprised to learn that this is your dressing.

When the microwave beeps, uncover and drain the cauliflower right away to avoid overcooking. Let it cool a little, so it doesn't cook all the other vegetables.

When the cauliflower has stopped steaming, add it to the bowl with the other veggies, pour on the dressing, and mix it all up. Season with salt to taste and you're done!

Yield: 6 servings

Per serving: 240 calories; 26g fat (89.1% calories from fat); 2g protein; 5g carbohydrate; 2g dietary fiber

Napa-Fennel-Pear Slaw
One of those recipes that just sort of occurred to me, this worked out beautifully. It's good with chicken, fish, or pork, especially if prepared with an Asian flavor accent.

8 cups (600 g) shredded napa cabbage

1 fennel bulb

1 bunch scallions

1 ripe but crisp pear

1 bunch fresh cilantro

½ cup (46 g) sliced almonds

1 tablespoon (14 g) bland coconut oil

¾ cup (175 ml) light olive oil

4 teaspoons (20 ml) lime juice

4 teaspoons (20 ml) rice vinegar

1 tablespoon (8 g) grated fresh ginger

6 drops liquid stevia

1 clove of garlic, crushed

1½ teaspoons dark sesame oil

1½ teaspoons fish sauce

¼ teaspoon sriracha sauce

Per serving: 261 calories; 22g fat **(84.9% calories from fat)***; 2g protein; 7g carbohydrate; 2g dietary fiber*

Slice the cabbage quite thin across the head and cut those long strips across a couple of times. Throw 'em into a big bowl.

Whack the stalk off the fennel bulb. Reserve the feathery leaves as a garnish. Quarter the bulb lengthwise and then slice it paper-thin. Add to the cabbage.

Slice the scallions thin and add those, too.

Cut the pear in quarters and remove the core. Then slice into matchstick strips. Add it to everything else! Mince the cilantro and throw it in, too.

In a small skillet, stir the almonds in the coconut oil over medium-low heat until they're touched with gold. Let cool.

Put all of the remaining ingredients into a blender and run until the garlic is pulverized and the mixture is uniform. Pour over the salad and toss till everything is well coated. Add the almonds, toss again, and chill.

Serve with a pretty frond or two of fennel leaves for garnish.

Yield: 10 servings

Ensalada de Col y Pepitas

I was looking for something new to pair with the Tex-Mex Pulled Pork on page 151—it can take two people a looong time to go through a pork shoulder—and came up with this. The pumpkin seeds really add interest.

1½ teaspoons coconut oil

½ cup (114 g) raw shelled pumpkin seeds

½ teaspoon salt, plus more as needed

½ a head green cabbage, sliced

⅓ cup (55 g) diced red onion

½ cup (115 g) sour cream

½ cup (115 g) mayonnaise

2 cloves of garlic, crushed

1½ teaspoons paprika (I use sweet, but use what you like.)

1 teaspoon Tabasco Chipotle sauce

⅓ cup (5 g) minced fresh cilantro

Per serving: 305 calories; 29g fat (79.3% calories from fat); 8g protein; 9g carbohydrate; 3g dietary fiber

First, in your medium skillet, melt the coconut oil over medium heat. Add the pumpkin seeds and stir them until they start to swell a little and turn golden. Sprinkle with the ½ teaspoon salt, stir it in, and remove from the heat.

Put the cabbage and onion into a large bowl.

Combine the sour cream, mayonnaise, garlic, paprika, and Tabasco. Stir it all up, pour it over the cabbage and onion, and toss till everything is evenly coated.

Add the cilantro and toasted pumpkin seeds. Taste and add salt if needed. Serve!

Yield: 6 servings

Pecan-Chipotle Slaw

This slaw is sweet, spicy, crunchy, fresh-tasting, and really unusual. It's so good. Lime juice would be good in place of the lemon juice, if you like. This would really dress up a simple roast chicken and would be killer with pork chops.

1 cup (100 g) pecans

½ a head green cabbage, shredded

1 carrot, shredded

1 Granny Smith apple, diced

½ a red onion, diced

2 tablespoons (12 g) chopped fresh mint

¾ cup (175 g) mayonnaise

1 tablespoon (15 g) brown mustard

6 drops liquid stevia

1 canned chipotle chile in adobo sauce

2 tablespoons (28 ml) lemon juice

Salt and ground black pepper

Preheat the oven to 350°F (180°C, or gas mark 4). Spread the pecans on a shallow baking pan and give them 6 minutes. Don't overcook! When they're done, let cool slightly and then chop.

Throw the cabbage, carrot, apple, onion, and mint into a large bowl.

Add the mayo, mustard, stevia, chipotle, and lemon juice to a blender or food processor and run till the chipotle is pulverized.

Pour it all over the veggies in the bowl and stir it up till everything is evenly mixed and coated. Stir in the pecans; then season with salt and pepper to taste. Serve or let it sit in the fridge for several hours for the flavors to blend.

Yield: 8 servings

Per serving: 258 calories; 27g fat ***(87% calories from fat)***; *2g protein; 7g carbohydrate; 2g dietary fiber*

Balsamic Vinaigrette

Why not just buy bottled vinaigrette dressing? Because the oil in those dressings is garbage, that's why. And this is super-easy, and tastes much better anyway.

½ cup (120 ml) olive oil

3 tablespoons (45 ml) balsamic vinegar

1 clove of garlic, peeled

½ teaspoon Dijon mustard

½ teaspoon dried oregano

¼ teaspoon salt

⅛ teaspoon ground black pepper

This is so easy! Put everything in the blender and run it or put it all in a clean old jar with a lid and shake like mad. If you do it in a jar, you can store any leftovers there, too.

Yield: ¾ cup (175 ml), or 6 servings

Per serving: 162 calories; 18g fat ***(97.9% calories from fat)***; *trace protein; 1g carbohydrate; trace dietary fiber*

Mexicali Dressing

I first made this to use on the Tex-Mex Pulled Pork Salad on page 118, but it's great on all kinds of things. Try it over a simple iceberg wedge or use it to marinate chicken or to tenderize a chuck roast.

½ cup (120 ml) extra-virgin olive oil

½ cup (120 ml) red wine vinegar

2 teaspoons brown mustard

1 teaspoon lime juice

½ teaspoon salt

½ teaspoon paprika

½ a clove of garlic, crushed

2 teaspoons finely minced onion

¼ teaspoon dried oregano

¼ teaspoon liquid stevia

¼ teaspoon Tabasco Chipotle sauce

You can do this in the blender or just in a clean jar with a tight-fitting lid—just put everything in and blend or shake until well mixed. Shake it again right before using.

Yield: 1 cup (235 ml), or 8 servings

Per serving: 124 calories; 14g fat **(95.6% calories from fat)**; *trace protein; 1g carbohydrate; trace dietary fiber*

Smoky Paprika Dressing

I came up with this dressing for the Chicken and Bell Pepper Salad on page 109, but it's good on all kinds of salads. Toss with cabbage for a fun twist on slaw or mix with cubed leftover pork roast, celery, a little diced red onion, and a touch of red apple for a summer supper.

3 tablespoons (45 ml) extra-virgin olive oil

3 tablespoons (42 g) mayonnaise

2 tablespoons (28 ml) sherry vinegar

1 teaspoon smoked paprika

Just combine everything! Feel free to double or triple.

Yield: ½ cup (115 g), or 4 servings

Per serving: 166 calories; 19g fat **(97.8% calories from fat)**; *trace protein; 1g carbohydrate; 0g dietary fiber*

Creamy Piquant Dressing

This one is for those of you who love Caesar salad but have quit dairy. Tester Burma says that she likes this better than her regular Caesar dressing recipe! Just toss with romaine.

1 egg yolk

2 tablespoons (28 ml) white wine vinegar

2 tablespoons (28 ml) lemon juice

1 clove of garlic, crushed

2 anchovy fillets

1 tablespoon (15 g) Dijon mustard

3 drops liquid stevia

⅓ cup (80 ml) olive oil

¼ cup (60 ml) coconut milk

¼ teaspoon salt

⅛ teaspoon ground black pepper

Put the egg yolk, vinegar, lemon juice, garlic, anchovies, mustard, and stevia in your blender and run till the anchovies are pulverized.

Leaving the blender running, slowly drizzle in the olive oil, then the coconut milk. When they're both worked in, add the salt and pepper, blend for another few seconds, and taste. Adjust the seasoning and then turn off the blender and either use your dressing or pour it into a clean jar with a tight-fitting lid.

Yield: 1½ cups (355 ml), or 12 servings

Per serving: 62 calories; 7g fat (93.2% calories from fat); 1g protein; 1g carbohydrate; trace dietary fiber

Ranch Dressing

Everybody loves ranch dressing, but like all the other prepared dressings in your grocery store, it's a bad-fat minefield. Here's how to make your own.

1 cup (225 g) mayonnaise

½ cup (115 g) sour cream

4 scallions, sliced

1 tablespoon (4 g) minced fresh parsley

1 tablespoon (4 g) minced fresh dill

1 clove of garlic, crushed

¼ teaspoon ground black pepper

⅛ teaspoon salt

Add all of the ingredients to your food processor and run till it's well-blended. Store in a jar in the fridge, of course.

NOTES: You can go with 1 teaspoon each of dried parsley and dried dill in place of the fresh herbs, but it won't be as flavorful.

This is thick, more the texture of a dip than a dressing. Thin it with a little buttermilk if you want something more pourable.

Yield: 1½ cups (360 g), or 12 servings

Per serving: 154 calories; 18g fat (96.3% calories from fat); 1g protein; 1g carbohydrate; trace dietary fiber

Bacon-Roasted Garlic Ranch Dressing
Every good dressing deserves a variation! And how can you ever go wrong with bacon?

3 cloves of garlic, unpeeled
1 tablespoon (14 g) bacon grease
½ cup (115 g) mayonnaise
½ cup (115 g) sour cream
½ cup (120 ml) buttermilk
2 teaspoons lemon juice
1 teaspoon cider vinegar
4 scallions, sliced
1 tablespoon (4 g) minced fresh parsley
1 tablespoon (4 g) minced fresh dill
¼ teaspoon salt
⅛ teaspoon ground black pepper

Preheat the oven to 350°F (180°C, or gas mark 4). Poke a hole in each garlic clove with the tip of a knife and put 'em in a little baking dish. Bake for 20 minutes; then let them cool.

Put all of the remaining ingredients in your blender or food processor. Peel the roasted garlic and throw the cloves in there, too. Run the blender or food processor until the garlic and scallions are pulverized.

Yield: 1½ cups (360 g), or 12 servings

Per serving: 103 calories; 11g fat **(91.8% calories from fat)**; *1g protein; 1g carbohydrate; trace dietary fiber*

Coleslaw Dressing
I've published versions of this recipe for years because it's been my favorite for years, because coleslaw is so popular, and because commercial coleslaw not only uses bad fats, but is also teeming with sugar. Think I exaggerate? A single serving of KFC coleslaw contains 19 grams of carbohydrate. How much of that do you think comes from the cabbage?

½ cup (115 g) sour cream
½ cup (115 g) mayonnaise
2 tablespoons (28 ml) cider vinegar
1 tablespoon (15 g) brown mustard
¼ teaspoon salt
Liquid stevia, as needed (I use about 12 drops.)

Just mix everything together and toss with shredded cabbage, bagged coleslaw mix, brocco-slaw, or what have you. I like coleslaw as a side with almost any simple meat or poultry.

Yield: 1 cup (240 g), or 8 servings

Per serving: 132 calories; 15g fat **(95.1% calories from fat)**; *1g protein; 1g carbohydrate; trace dietary fiber*

Another Poppy Seed Dressing

Poppy seed dressing is very popular, especially for any salad that includes fruit, but the commercial ones not only contain questionable oils, but also lots of sugar. Make this healthy, delicious version instead.

¼ cup (60 ml) oil (I use MCT oil or sunflower oil, but light olive oil would work, too.)

2 tablespoons (28 ml) cider vinegar

¼ teaspoon liquid stevia

¼ teaspoon Worcestershire sauce

1 teaspoon minced onion

¼ teaspoon paprika

1 tablespoon (9 g) poppy seeds

1½ teaspoons sesame seeds

*Per serving: 187 calories; 20g fat **(94.4% calories from fat)**; 1g protein; 2g carbohydrate; 1g dietary fiber*

Put the oil, vinegar, stevia, Worcestershire sauce, onion, and paprika in your food processor or blender and run for 15 seconds or so to pulverize the onion. Add the poppy and sesame seeds, run for just a second to mix them in (but not pulverize them!), and turn off the machine. Pour into a jar with a lid and chill for 1 hour or more. Shake before using.

NOTE: Burma, who tested this with the Asparagus-Strawberry Salad on page 84, said that it was worthy of its own entry. She also says that she might like it a tiny bit better with only 2 teaspoons of poppy seeds, but the other diners thought the poppy seed concentration was perfect. So the question is, how much do you like poppy seeds?

Yield: 3 servings

Vegetables and Other Hot Side Dishes

'm using the term *side dishes* loosely here. On the one hand, these can be a great way to add fat to a meal built around a lower-fat protein source, like chicken or fish. On the other hand, these recipes are tasty and filling enough to be satisfying in their own right. If you've already had enough protein for the day, one of these dishes might be the perfect supper.

You can, of course, simply steam the vegetables and serve them with butter, hollandaise, aioli, or the like, and you'll have a low-carb, high-fat dish. Too, it is a rare vegetable that doesn't benefit from being tossed with some oil or bacon grease and roasted at a high temperature—400 to 500°F (200 to 250°C, or gas marks 6 to 10), stirring occasionally—until browned. Asparagus, cauliflower, turnips, Brussels sprouts, broccoli, rutabaga, and more all benefit from this sort of treatment.

Zoodles

These zucchini "noodles" have taken the low-carb and paleo world by storm, and with good reason. They're terrific and quick! Try them with any type of pasta sauce. You'll need a spiral slicer to make these; they run around $30 and are very simple to use. You'll want to buy a zucchini with a slightly smaller diameter than the spiral slicer.

1 medium zucchini

3 tablespoons (45 ml) olive oil or (42 g) butter

Salt (optional)

Per serving: 193 calories; 20g fat (92% calories from fat); 1g protein; 3g carbohydrate; 1g dietary fiber

Just run the zucchini through the slicer, reducing it to a pile of long, skinny strips. Now you have a choice:

You can, if you have 20 minutes, salt the zoodles liberally and let them sit for that long. When the 20 minutes are up, use clean hands to squeeze them dry. Discard the water. This step renders your zoodles more limp and noodle-like. However, I have skipped straight to the next step and found the results quite tasty.

Put your big skillet over medium heat and add the oil or butter or a combo of the two. Let it get hot. Then throw in the zoodles and sauté, stirring constantly, for about 5 minutes. That's it!

NOTE: You can vary these easily, of course, by adding a little crushed garlic to the fat you fry them in, or throwing in some herbs, or sautéing a little onion for a minute before adding the zoodles. Play around with it!

Yield: 2 servings

Mixed Mash

Pureed cauliflower, fondly called "fauxtatoes," is a low-carb staple. Adding celeriac, aka celery root, to the mix, however, gives it a texture closer to mashed potatoes. This is really good.

12 ounces (340 g) celeriac

¼ a head of cauliflower (Trim the very bottom stem.)

3 tablespoons (42 g) butter

1½ ounces (43 g) cream cheese

Salt and ground black pepper

Per serving: 149 calories; 13g fat (73.4% calories from fat); 2g protein; 8g carbohydrate; 2g dietary fiber

Celeriac is an ugly, knobby thing. You'll need to scrub it well and peel it with a knife, not a vegetable peeler, as there will be divots of toughness folding down into the flesh. When you've got it peeled, cut it into cubes.

Steam the celiac cubes until soft—I'd put them in a microwave-able casserole dish or microwave steamer, add a few tablespoons (45 to 60 ml) of water, cover, and nuke on High for 10 minutes or so and then check. You may also steam them on the stovetop.

(continued on page 96)

Mixed Mash

(continued from page 95)

While the celeriac is cooking, cut the cauliflower into chunks, too. When the microwave beeps, add the cauliflower to the celeriac and let the whole thing steam for another 10 minutes or so. You want both to be soft.

Drain well and then dump the celeriac and cauliflower into your food processor. Add the butter and cream cheese and run the processor until you have a silky-smooth puree. Season with salt and pepper to taste and serve.

Yield: 4 servings

Broccoli with Cashews
This recipe has a clear Chinese influence, with an American accent. And, of course, it omits the cornstarch and sugar so often found in Americanized Chinese food.

1 pound (455 g) broccoli

3 tablespoons (42 g) butter

2 tablespoons (28 ml) soy sauce

1½ teaspoons rice vinegar

6 drops liquid stevia (English toffee flavor)

1 clove of garlic, minced

¼ teaspoon ground black pepper

¼ cup (35 g) chopped roasted, salted cashews

Per serving: 199 calories; 17g fat (72.1% calories from fat); 5g protein; 10g carbohydrate; 4g dietary fiber

Cut the broccoli into bite-size bits. Don't toss the stems; peel the tough skin off and cut them into bits, too. They're the best part!

Steam it till just tender-crisp—I'd put it in my microwave steamer, add a little water, cover, and give it 5 minutes on High and then check to see if it needed 1 or 2 more minutes. You may also steam it on the stovetop.

While your broccoli is cooking, melt the butter in a small saucepan and whisk in the soy sauce, vinegar, stevia, garlic, and pepper.

When the broccoli is tender-crisp and brilliant green, drain it and toss in a bowl with your sauce. Add the cashews, toss again and then serve.

Yield: 3 servings

Amazing Brussels Sprouts
The first time I made these, I practically had to leave the house so as not to eat them all up before That Nice Boy I Married came home.

¼ cup (56 g) bacon grease
1 pound (455 g) Brussels sprouts
¼ cup (28 g) chopped pecans

Per serving: 170 calories; 15g fat (74.1% calories from fat); 3g protein; 8g carbohydrate; 4g dietary fiber

Preheat the oven to 400°F (200°C, or gas mark 6). Put the bacon grease in a roasting pan (heavy dark metal is best) and stick it in the oven to melt while the oven heats.

Trim the bottoms of the stems and any wilted leaves from the Brussels sprouts and then quarter them. When the grease is melted, add the Brussels sprouts to the pan and stir them up till they're all coated with the bacon grease. Stick 'em in the oven and set a timer for 10 minutes.

Stir your Brussels and put them back in the oven for another 10 minutes. Stir up the Brussels again. They should be starting to brown. If not, give them another 5 minutes. When they're getting brown, stir in the pecans and put them back in the oven. This time, set the timer for 5 minutes.

Stir your sprouts once again and give them another 3 to 5 minutes. They should be starting to get pretty dark brown and crispy—but don't burn the pecans! Serve ASAP, that is, if you don't stand over the stove and eat them all out of the pan.

Yield: 5 servings

About Brussels Sprouts

The first time I tried Brussels sprouts was a terrible disappointment. I love cabbage, so I expected to love Brussels sprouts, too. I simply boiled and buttered them, only to find that they were bitter and nasty. They tasted like I imagine nail polish remover would. I gave up on the whole idea of Brussels sprouts.

Then we visited some friends who served us Brussels sprouts fried in olive oil until they were dark brown. They were not merely good, but addictive. Since then I have learned that I love Brussels sprouts pretty much any way but boiled and buttered.

So please, if traumatic childhood experience has left you convinced that you loathe Brussels sprouts, give them at least one more try. You might find, as we have, that they're the new favorite vegetable.

Skillet Bacon-Walnut Brussels

If you've never tried slicing and sautéing Brussels sprouts, you simply must. It turns them into almost a different vegetable! And what with the walnuts and bacon—as my mom would have said, what could be bad?

5 bacon slices

½ cup (60 g) chopped walnuts

1 pound (455 g) Brussels sprouts

2 tablespoons (28 g) bacon grease

1 tablespoon (15 ml) balsamic vinegar

1 teaspoon brown mustard

Per serving: 245 calories; 20g fat (67.7% calories from fat); 10g protein; 11g carbohydrate; 5g dietary fiber

In a big, heavy skillet over medium heat, start cooking the bacon.

Put the walnuts in your food processor and pulse till they're chopped to a medium consistency. Dump them out into a bowl and swap the S-blade for the slicing disk. Don't forget to turn the bacon!

Trim the bottoms of the stems from the Brussels sprouts and remove any wilted leaves. Run them through the slicing blade of your food processor.

When the bacon is crisp, transfer it to a plate and add the walnuts to the skillet. Sauté them for 5 minutes or so. Scoop them out with a slotted spoon, back into the bowl.

Add the Brussels sprouts to the skillet, along with the extra bacon grease, and cook them, stirring every few minutes, until they're softened and turning brown.

When the Brussels are done, crumble in the bacon and stir in the walnuts. Stir the vinegar and mustard together and then stir that in, too. Toss everything together till it's evenly combined and serve.

Yield: 4 servings

Crispy Brussels Sprouts

These are so exotic! The soy sauce, lime, fish sauce, and sriracha are all Asian, of course, while Brussels sprouts, as the name strongly suggests, are European in origin. It's sort of East-meets-West.

1 pound (455 g) Brussels sprouts
⅓ cup (75 g) lard or coconut oil
2 tablespoons (28 ml) soy sauce
4½ teaspoons (23 ml) lime juice
1 tablespoon (15 ml) fish sauce
10 drops liquid stevia
2 teaspoons sriracha sauce
1 clove of garlic, crushed

Per serving: 210 calories; 18g fat (71.4% calories from fat); 4g protein; 11g carbohydrate; 4g dietary fiber

Trim the bottoms of the stems and any bruised leaves off of the Brussels sprouts. Run them through the slicing blade of your food processor.

In your big, heavy skillet, melt the lard over medium heat. Sauté the Brussels sprouts until they're brown and getting crispy.

Meanwhile, stir together all of the remaining ingredients.

When the Brussels are browned and crispy, pour in the seasonings and stir them in. Keep cooking until the sauce mostly evaporates and then serve.

Yield: 4 servings

Buttery Cabbage with Walnuts

I love cabbage! It's delicious, nutritious, low-carb, versatile, and consistently cheap. Furthermore, it keeps for a long time in the fridge, making it convenient. You owe it to yourself to have cabbage in the fridge all the time.

4 tablespoons (55 g) butter, divided
½ cup (60 g) chopped walnuts
2 shallots, minced
½ a head of green cabbage, thinly sliced
Salt and ground black pepper

Per serving: 152 calories; 14g fat (76.1% calories from fat); 4g protein; 6g carbohydrate; 2g dietary fiber

Put your big, heavy skillet over medium-low heat and melt half of the butter. Throw in the walnuts and stir them in the butter until they smell toasty, about 5 minutes. Scoop them out, put them on a plate, and reserve.

Turn up the burner a little— no higher than medium— and melt the rest of the butter. Add the shallots and sauté for just a minute or so and then add the cabbage. Cook till the cabbage is just tender.

Season with salt and pepper to taste, stir in the reserved walnuts, and serve.

Yield: 6 servings

Roasted Cremini Mushrooms

My tester Soren says, "Wow! My kitchen smells like a French bistro! Very easy: Just wipe, toss, roast. And they taste *phenomenal*, with hardly any effort."

2 pounds (900 g) cremini mushrooms

3 cloves of garlic, crushed

½ cup (120 ml) olive oil

2 tablespoons (28 ml) dry white wine

2 tablespoons (8 g) minced fresh parsley

2 teaspoons salt

½ teaspoon ground black pepper

Per serving: 202 calories; 19g fat (79.7% calories from fat); 3g protein; 7g carbohydrate; 2g dietary fiber

Preheat the oven to 400°F (200°C, or gas mark 6).

Wipe the mushrooms clean with a damp paper towel and put them in a big bowl.

Mix together everything else and pour it over the mushrooms. Stir it all up till it's quite well acquainted.

Spread in a single layer in a baking dish. Bake for 20 to 25 minutes, basting once or twice with the liquid in the pan. Serve hot.

NOTE: Soren says these mushrooms would be good without the parsley, (I just always keep parsley on hand) and that any fresh herbs you have around would be good, or, for that matter, none at all. She also says to go for dry sherry or red wine if you don't have white wine in the house.

Yield: 6 servings

Gorgonzola Mushrooms

I had this over shirataki and it was top-notch, but it would also be wonderful over a steak or in an omelet—or just as a side dish.

3 tablespoons (42 g) butter

¼ cup (40 g) diced onion

8 ounces (255 g) sliced mushrooms

1 clove of garlic, crushed

1½ tablespoons (4 g) minced fresh sage, or 1½ teaspoons dried sage

¼ cup (60 ml) heavy cream

½ cup (60 g) crumbled Gorgonzola cheese

Salt and ground black pepper

In a medium-size skillet over medium heat, melt the butter and start sautéing the onion and mushrooms. I break my mushrooms up further with the edge of my spatula as I sauté because I like the smaller bits, but leave them in slices if you prefer. (Why don't I just chop my mushrooms? Because I buy them already sliced.)

When the onion is translucent and the mushrooms have softened and changed color, stir in the garlic, sage, cream, and Gorgonzola. Stir it all around until most of the cheese is melted, but leave a few chunks, for texture and an explosion of Gorg-y flavor in your mouth!

Season with salt and pepper to taste and serve.

*Per serving: 337 calories; 32g fat **(80% calories from fat)**; 11g protein; 7g carbohydrate; 1g dietary fiber*

NOTE: *You could use a different blue cheese in this, if you like. I just think the mild and creamy Gorgonzola works beautifully.*

Yield: 3 servings

Hongos Chipotles

So there I was with a bunch of mushroom stems left over from making stuffed mushrooms. This is what became of them, and it's easily delicious enough to buy mushrooms just for the purpose.

2 cups (140 g) sliced mushrooms or mushroom stems

3 tablespoons (42 g) coconut oil or lard

2 cloves of garlic, crushed

1 teaspoon ground cumin

1 tablespoon (15 ml) Tabasco Chipotle sauce

2 tablespoons (2 g) minced fresh cilantro (optional)

In a skillet over medium heat, sauté the mushrooms in the coconut oil or lard until they're softening. Stir in the garlic, cumin, and Tabasco and let it cook for another few minutes. Stir in the minced cilantro, if you're using it. Now serve as a side dish, or spread it on a steak or piece of chicken, or use it to fill an omelet (great with Monterey Jack).

Yield: 4 servings

*Per serving: 102 calories; 10g fat **(87.1% calories from fat)**; 1g protein; 3g carbohydrate; 1g dietary fiber*

Mustard-Maple Glazed Turnips

These are really good anytime, but are certainly worthy of serving at a holiday dinner. If you can afford a few more carbs, try this with rutabaga, too.

3 tablespoons (42 g) coconut oil

4 turnips, each about the size of a baseball

4 tablespoons (55 g) Maple Butter (page 49)

2 teaspoons brown mustard

*Per serving: 327 calories; 34g fat **(89% calories from fat)**; 2g protein; 8g carbohydrate; 2g dietary fiber*

Preheat the oven to 350°F (180°C, or gas mark 4). While it's heating, put the coconut oil in a baking pan and slide it into the oven to melt.

Peel the turnips and cut them into chunks. I suggest pieces measuring about ½ × 1½ inches (1.3 × 3.8 cm).

Toss the turnips in the coconut oil, coating them all over. Put the baking pan back in the oven and set a timer for 15 minutes.

When the timer beeps, stir up the turnips, using a spatula to turn them over so they brown evenly. Give them another 15 minutes in the oven. Repeat the stirring/turning-over routine and give them yet another 15 minutes.

By now the turnips should be softened and getting browned all over. Stir in the Maple Butter and mustard. Give your turnips another 10 to 15 minutes and serve.

Yield: 4 servings

Sautéed Green Beans with Tarragon

I've fallen in love with tarragon recently, and here it gives the beans what I imagine to be a French air. Call 'em *haricots verts* if you like.

1 pound (455 g) green beans

2 tablespoons (28 g) butter

2 tablespoons (28 ml) olive oil

1 shallot, finely minced

½ teaspoon dried tarragon

1 tablespoon (15 ml) dry white wine

Per serving: 146 calories; 13g fat (74.6% calories from fat); 2g protein; 8g carbohydrate; 3g dietary fiber

Pinch the ends off the green beans. Cut them into shorter lengths if you want to, though I don't.

Put your big, heavy skillet over medium-high heat. Add the butter and olive oil and swirl them together as the butter melts.

Add the green beans and sauté till they've turned brilliantly green. Add the shallot and keep sautéing for another few minutes.

Stir in the tarragon and wine. Turn the burner down to medium-low, cover the skillet, and let the whole thing cook for another 4 to 5 minutes, till the beans are just tender, and then serve.

Yield: 4 servings

Mushroom-Parmesan Pilaf

Here's just one demonstration of the myriad of ways that cauli-rice can stand in for grains in all kinds of dishes. A tip of my hat to Fran McCullough for the original idea, in her book *The Low-Carb Cookbook*. So far as I know, she originated the idea of shredded, steamed cauliflower as a rice substitute. I've been playing with it ever since, in everything from side dishes to salads.

½ a head of cauliflower (Trim the very bottom stem.)

4 tablespoons (55 g) butter

2 tablespoons (28 ml) extra-virgin olive oil

8 ounces (225 g) cremini mushrooms, sliced

½ cup (80 g) diced onion

2 cloves of garlic, crushed

¼ cup (60 ml) dry white wine

½ teaspoon ground black pepper

¼ cup (25 g) shredded Parmesan cheese

Per serving: 156 calories; 13g fat (76.4% calories from fat); 3g protein; 6g carbohydrate; 2g dietary fiber

Trim the cauliflower, whack it into chunks, and run it through the shredding blade of your food processor. Put the resulting cauli-rice in a microwaveable casserole with a lid (if it's a round casserole, a plate works fine as a lid) or a microwave steamer. Add a couple of tablespoons (28 ml) of water, cover, and nuke on High for 8 minutes. When the microwave beeps, uncover the cauli-rice.

In the meanwhile, melt the butter in your big heavy skillet over medium heat. Add the olive oil and swirl together. Throw in the mushrooms, onion, and garlic and sauté until the mushrooms have changed color and softened and the onion is translucent.

Pour in the wine, add the pepper, and cook till most of the wine has evaporated. Stir in the cauli-rice. Just before serving, stir in the Parmesan.

Yield: 6 servings

The First Eggplant My Husband Really, Really Liked

The title of this recipe is for real. That Nice Boy I Married was not enthusiastic about eggplant until I cooked it this way. Then he yummed down slice after slice. It's super-easy, too. The measurements for this are loose. I don't know how big your eggplant will be, nor exactly how much olive oil it will suck up. However, eggplant is very low-carb, and it seems to have a nearly unlimited ability to absorb oil, making it ideal for a low-carb/high-fat side dish.

1 medium-size globe eggplant
1 cup (235 ml) olive oil
Salt and ground black pepper

Per serving: 338 calories; 36g fat (93.8% calories from fat); 1g protein; 5g carbohydrate; 2g dietary fiber

This is easy: Slice the eggplant across, into big rounds between ½ and ¾ inch (1.3 and 1.9 cm) thick. Put your big skillet over medium heat and add ¼ inch (6 mm) of the olive oil. Let it get hot and then fry the eggplant till it's golden on either side, adding more oil as needed.

Serve hot with salt and pepper. That's it—the sum total of the recipe.

NOTE: Some people like to salt their eggplant slices for a half an hour or so before frying them. They say this gets rid of bitterness or some such thing. I haven't run across a bitter eggplant yet, but I'm sure it could happen. Do as you see fit.

Yields: 6 servings

Pepperoni–Pine Nut Shirataki

Wow. I've put this recipe with the side dishes, but confess that I ate the whole batch myself as a simple supper. As a side dish, it will serve two.

1 packet tofu shirataki (I use spaghetti-width.)
1 ounce (28 g) pepperoni slices
2 tablespoons (28 ml) olive oil
2 tablespoons (18 g) pine nuts
2 cloves of garlic, crushed
1 tablespoon (4 g) minced fresh parsley
¼ teaspoon red pepper flakes
Salt and ground black pepper

Do the whole drain-rinse-nuke thing with the shirataki (see page 24). While the noodles are in the microwave, cut the pepperoni slices into ¼-inch (6 mm) strips. Put them in a medium-size heavy skillet over medium heat and start frying them; you want them to become crispy.

When the pepperoni is crispy, scoop it out onto a plate, leaving the grease that cooked out in the skillet.

Add the oil and pine nuts to the skillet and sauté till the pine nuts have a few golden spots. Scoop out the pine nuts and stash them with the pepperoni strips.

(continued on page 105)

Pepperoni-Pine Nut Shirataki
(continued from page 104)

*If you eat it all yourself, you'll get: 487 calories; 48g fat (**87.2% calories from fat**); 11g protein; 5g carbohydrate; 1g dietary fiber*

Add the garlic, parsley, and red pepper flakes to the oil in the skillet. Drain the shirataki one more time and then add it to the skillet and toss it with the oil and seasonings. Make sure it's all evenly coated. Season with salt and pepper and pile the shirataki on a plate or in a bowl. Top with the pepperoni and pine nuts and serve.

NOTES: You can sprinkle a little Parmesan on this if you like, but it's not essential.

Feel free to make this with Zoodles (page 95) instead of the shirataki.

Yield: 2 servings

Mushroom and Artichoke Sauté
I used canned artichoke hearts in this recipe because I had them on hand, but feel free to use frozen ones, thawed of course. This is great by itself as a side, or turn it into a meal with a couple of fried eggs on top, or some diced cooked chicken, or even crumbled, browned Italian sausage mixed in.

⅓ cup (75 g) coconut oil or lard

½ cup (80 g) diced onion

8 ounces (255 g) sliced mushrooms (I buy 'em that way!)

14 ounces (390 g) canned artichoke hearts, drained and chopped

3 tablespoons (45 ml) dry sherry

2 teaspoons dried rosemary

½ teaspoon anchovy paste

Salt and ground black pepper

Per serving: 232 calories; 19g fat (73.4% calories from fat); 4g protein; 11g carbohydrate; 1g dietary fiber

Set your big skillet over medium-low heat, melt the coconut oil and start sautéing the onion. Throw the mushrooms in, too. When the onions and mushrooms have softened, stir in the artichoke hearts, sherry, rosemary, and anchovy paste. Season with salt and pepper to taste and serve.

Yield: 4 servings

Crunchy Eggplant

This is the second eggplant dish my husband really, really liked. I think I'm on a roll here. I liked the leftovers warmed up in a skillet (reheating in the microwave would leave the coating dispirited) and topped with fried eggs for breakfast.

1 medium-size globe eggplant

Salt

¼ cup (28 g) coconut flour

1 large egg

2 teaspoons water

1 cup (120 g) pork rind crumbs, made from barbecue flavor pork rinds

½ cup (112 g) bacon grease, or more as needed

Per serving: 462 calories; 36g fat (69.5% calories from fat); 18g protein; 18g carbohydrate; 9g dietary fiber

Slice the eggplant about ¼ inch (6 mm) thick. Sprinkle both sides of each slice lightly with salt and let it sit for 20 to 30 minutes.

In the meanwhile, set up a little assembly line: a plate with the coconut flour, a plate with the egg beaten up with the water, and a plate with the pork rind crumbs.

Put your big, heavy skillet over medium heat and add the bacon grease.

Pat a slice of eggplant dry (it will have exuded a bit of moisture). Dip both sides in the coconut flour, then the egg wash, and then the pork rind crumbs. You should get a fairly heavy coating.

Fry your crumb-coated eggplant in the hot grease until brown and crisp on both sides, adding more bacon grease as needed. Continue until you run out of eggplant. Serve hot; it's better to have folks eating the first slices while more are frying than to let 'em get soggy.

NOTE: These quantities are approximate; I wound up with a little leftover egg and crumbs, but I added a couple of tablespoons (28 g) of extra bacon grease to the skillet. It all depends on the size of your eggplant.

Yield: 4 servings

Hot, Crunchy Avocado

Why didn't I try this before? Only recently have I discovered the joys of hot cooked avocados. They're wonderful, and this is a really unusual and delicious dish.

1 avocado

3 tablespoons (21 g) coconut flour, plus more for dusting

1 large egg

2 teaspoons water

1 cup (120 g) pork rind crumbs, made from barbecue flavor pork rinds

½ cup (112 g) coconut oil

Per serving: 661 calories; 59g fat (77.5% calories from fat); 23g protein; 16g carbohydrate; 8g dietary fiber

Halve the avocado and slice it ½ inch (1.3 cm) thick. Remove the skin from the slices. Dust the slices with coconut flour.

On a rimmed plate, mix the egg with the water until blended. On another plate, combine the coconut flour and pork rind crumbs.

Dip the avocado slices in the egg wash, then in the pork rind crumbs, covering the whole surface.

When the avocado slices are all "breaded," let them sit while you heat your big, heavy skillet over medium heat; if it's not nonstick, you might want to give it a squirt of cooking spray, but it's not essential. Melt the coconut oil in the skillet.

When the fat is hot, add the avocado slices, taking care not to splash the fat. Let them fry for 3 minutes or so till the bottoms are crunchy. Flip and fry the other side. Serve hot!

NOTE: You're not likely to use exactly all the coconut flour, pork rind crumbs, or coconut oil, so an exact count is impossible. They'll be somewhat lower in calories and fat than these counts suggest, but they'll still be high in fat—and ultra-tasty.

Yield: 3 servings

VEGETABLES AND OTHER HOT SIDE DISHES

107

Main-Dish Salads

CHAPTER 7

You know how you can tell I started developing recipes for this book during the summer? There are lots of main-dish salad recipes. So long as it is temperate outside, there is nothing I like better; I could eat them every day, and often do.

When we talk about salads, we inevitably come to the issue of vegetables, and particularly of conventionally versus organically grown. I wish I could afford to buy all organic vegetables, but my budget doesn't go that far. I take my cues from the Dirty Dozen and Clean 15 lists created by the Environmental Working Group (easily found online) and buy organic lettuce, spinach, peppers, apples, and celery, but I cheap out and buy conventionally grown cabbage, cauliflower, and avocados.

Avocado-Egg Salad

Avocados and eggs may just be the world's most perfect flavor and texture combination. It's sheer joy on a hot summer afternoon, or evening, or, heck, eat this for breakfast; you'll be full all day.

2 large hard-boiled eggs

1 small tomato

½ an avocado

2 scallions

2 tablespoons (2 g) minced fresh cilantro

2 tablespoons (30 g) sour cream

2 tablespoons (28 g) mayonnaise

1 tablespoon (15 ml) lime juice

½ teaspoon hot pepper sauce

Salt

Dice up the eggs, tomato, and avocado and slice the scallions. Put it all in a big bowl.

Stir together everything else but the salt. This is, of course, your dressing. Pour over the salad and stir gently—you don't want to smash the avocado. Season with salt to taste and serve.

Yield: 2 servings

Per serving: 308 calories; 28g fat (77.4% calories from fat); 9g protein; 10g carbohydrate; 2g dietary fiber

Chicken and Bell Pepper Salad

This is a nice balance between leafy goodness, yummy chicken, nutty crunch, and the smoky tang of the paprika. I've been known to go buy a rotisserie chicken just to make this.

⅓ cup (37 g) slivered almonds

1 tablespoon (15 ml) olive oil

12 cups (660 g) mixed chopped lettuce

Smoky Paprika Dressing (page 90)

¼ of a red onion, sliced paper-thin

½ a red bell pepper, diced

2 cups (280 g) diced cooked chicken

Put your medium skillet over medium-low heat and start sautéing the slivered almonds in the olive oil. Don't walk away! Those almonds will burn on you the moment your back is turned. Just stir them until they're getting a little golden and then take them off the heat.

Pile the lettuce in a salad bowl, pour on the Smokey Paprika Dressing, and toss till it's all coated. Add the onion, bell pepper, and chicken and toss again.

Pile the salad onto 4 plates and divide the almonds among them. Serve!

Yield: 4 servings

Per serving: 549 calories; 46g fat (73.9% calories from fat); 26g protein; 11g carbohydrate; 5g dietary fiber

Chicken Salad Basilico

My neighbors Keith and Peter are the Organic Gardening Gods. (This is not an exaggeration, as they publish *Permaculture Activist* magazine.) All summer long, Keith shows up at my door with amazing produce and always, always huge, fragrant bouquets of fresh basil. How could I remain uninspired?

1 clove of garlic, crushed

¼ cup (60 ml) extra-virgin olive oil

¼ of a head of cauliflower (Trim the very bottom stem.)

2 tablespoons (18 g) pine nuts

¼ cup (40 g) diced red onion

¼ cup (10 g) minced fresh basil

¼ cup (25 g) chopped olives (I use half black and half green, good ones from the international grocery, but use what you have.)

2 tablespoons (14 g) chopped olive oil–packed sun-dried tomatoes

½ cup (70 g) diced cooked chicken

2 tablespoons (28 ml) red wine vinegar

Salt and ground black pepper

2 tablespoons (10 g) shredded Parmesan cheese

Per serving: 475 calories; 44g fat **(80.7% calories from fat);** *16g protein; 8g carbohydrate; 2g dietary fiber*

Crush the garlic and put it in a small bowl. Add the olive oil and let that sit while you assemble the rest of the salad.

Cut the cauliflower into chunks and run them through the shredding blade of a food processor. Put the resulting cauli-rice in a microwaveable bowl, add a couple of teaspoons of water, and cover the bowl; I would use a cereal bowl covered with a saucer for this amount of cauli-rice. Microwave on High for 4 to 5 minutes.

When the microwave beeps, uncover your cauli-rice immediately to stop the cooking. Don't let it get mushy! Drain it and dump it into a bowl. You want to let it cool a bit before you add the other stuff.

Stir the pine nuts in a small dry skillet over low heat for a few minutes until they're lightly golden.

Okay, it's time to assemble your salad! Add the onion, basil, olives, sun-dried tomatoes, chicken, and pine nuts to the cauliflower. Pour on the garlic-infused olive oil and stir everything up quite well. Add the vinegar and stir it up again. Season with salt and pepper to taste.

Pile your salad on 2 plates and top each serving with half of the Parmesan. Serve!

Yield: 2 servings

Chicken-Bacon-Avocado Salad

This is what happens when I have a few stray slices of bacon and a ripe avocado begging to be used up, plus chipotle mayo in the fridge. It's fabulous, beautiful, and super-filling. As I write this, it's five hours since I ate this salad, and I'm still stuffed.

¼ of a head of cauliflower (Trim the very bottom stem.)

5 bacon slices

¼ cup (40 g) diced red onion

1 medium tomato, diced

¼ of a medium green bell pepper, diced

1 cup (140 g) diced cooked chicken

¼ cup (4 g) minced fresh cilantro, plus a few leaves for garnish (optional)

½ cup (115 g) Chipotle Mayonnaise (page 45)

1 avocado, peeled and diced

Salt and ground black pepper

Hot pepper sauce of your choice

Per serving: 705 calories; 65g fat **(81.1% calories from fat);** *22g protein; 12g carbohydrate; 4g dietary fiber*

Whack the cauliflower into chunks and run it through the shredding blade of your food processor. Steam the shreds till just tender; I give mine 5 minutes on High in my microwave steamer.

When the microwave beeps, pull out the cauli-rice and uncover it right away to keep it from overcooking. Drain it and let it cool a bit; stirring now and then lets out steam and speeds the cooling process.

Cook the bacon—I give mine 8 minutes on High in the microwave, but you can cook yours however you like, so long as it's nice and crisp.

Okay, the cauli-rice is now just warm, and the bacon is crisp. Dump the cauli-rice into a big bowl. Add the red onion, tomato, bell pepper, diced chicken, and cilantro. Add the Chipotle Mayonnaise and stir till everything's friendly.

At the last minute before serving, halve, peel, and dice the avocado. Add it to the salad and crumble in the bacon. Stir, season with salt and pepper to taste, and see if you want a little hot sauce. (I do, but I'm a chilehead.) Serve! Garnish it with a few cilantro leaves, if you're feeling fancy.

Yield: 3 servings

111

Vaguely Asian Chicken Salad

Mayonnaise is definitely not Asian (though the Japanese seem to have a fondness for it). But you've got soy sauce, sesame oil, sriracha, and ginger to make up for that. And regardless, this tastes great!

1 cup (140 g) diced cooked chicken

½ cup (60 g) diced celery

½ cup (75 g) diced red or yellow bell pepper

3 scallions, sliced

⅓ cup (75 g) mayonnaise

1 tablespoon (15 ml) soy sauce

1 teaspoon grated fresh ginger

6 drops liquid stevia

½ teaspoon dark sesame oil

½ a clove of garlic, crushed

½ teaspoon sriracha sauce

⅓ cup (33 g) chopped wasabi-roasted almonds

Per serving: 687 calories; 62g fat (78.3% calories from fat); 28g protein; 11g carbohydrate; 4g dietary fiber

This recipe is pretty straightforward: Throw the chicken, celery, bell pepper, and scallions into a bowl.

Stir together the mayo, soy sauce, ginger, liquid stevia, sesame oil, garlic, and sriracha; pour over your assembled ingredients and toss to coat.

Either stir in the wasabi almonds or use them to top each serving and you're done!

NOTES: I almost added cilantro to this, but then I thought, "Geez, Dana, you add cilantro to everything, and not everyone likes it." So I didn't, and it was an admirable salad without it. But you could add cilantro if you're fond of it; it would definitely fit.

Wasabi-roasted almonds are available in cans in the nut aisle of your grocery store. My husband had put some in my Christmas stocking, and they were the inspiration for this recipe. But if you don't like wasabi, plain old roasted, salted almonds will do.

Yield: 2 servings

Mediterranean Chicken Salad

Do you have any idea how much of what ends up in my books is a product of what's in my fridge, waiting to be used up? I had leftover chicken, a quarter of a head of cauliflower, and some lemon-artichoke pesto, all staring at me hopefully. So I turned them into this. FYI, an easy way to pit an olive is to press down on it with your thumb; the pit can then be flicked right out.

¼ of a head of cauliflower (Trim the very bottom stem.)

1½ cups (210 g) diced cooked chicken

¼ cup (15 g) minced fresh parsley

12 kalamata olives, pitted and chopped

¼ cup (40 g) diced red onion

1 tablespoon (9 g) chopped capers

2 tablespoons (18 g) pine nuts

⅓ cup (87 g) Lemon-Artichoke Pesto (page 48)

¼ cup (60 ml) extra-virgin olive oil

½ teaspoon anchovy paste

1 tablespoon (15 ml) lemon juice

Salt and ground black pepper

Per serving: 680 calories; 53g fat (69.6% calories from fat); 40g protein; 12g carbohydrate; 3g dietary fiber

First, run the cauliflower through the shredding blade of your food processor, throw it into a microwaveable bowl (I use a cereal bowl), add a tablespoon (15 ml) or so of water, cover it with a saucer, and nuke it on High for 4 minutes.

Put the chicken, parsley, olives, onion, and capers in a bowl.

Somewhere in here your microwave will beep. Uncover the cauliflower to let out the steam and stop the cooking. Drain it and let it cool a bit.

While the cauliflower is cooling, put the pine nuts in a dry skillet over medium-low heat and stir them until they're touched with gold.

Put the Lemon-Artichoke Pesto, olive oil, anchovy paste, and lemon juice in a jar. Screw the lid on tightly and shake it vigorously.

Okay, the cauliflower is cool enough to not cook the parsley and onion. Add it to the bowl and stir the whole thing up. Pour on the dressing and stir again till everything is evenly coated. Season with salt and pepper to taste. Stir in the pine nuts and serve.

You can make this ahead and refrigerate it if you like, but it's best at room temperature or a little warmer, so get it out of the fridge a little while before you plan to eat it.

Yield: 2 servings

Orange-Cashew-Chicken Salad

This started with a recipe that called for a can of sweetened mandarin oranges. That wasn't happening in my kitchen, but the flavor combination was tantalizing, so I winged it. If you make this ahead, don't add the cashews till right before serving, or they'll get soggy.

½ an orange

½ cup (120 ml) light olive oil

¼ cup (60 ml) rice vinegar

¼ cup (60 ml) soy sauce

6 drops liquid stevia

2 teaspoons grated fresh ginger

1 clove of garlic, crushed

1 tablespoon (15 ml) dry sherry

8 ounces (225 g) cooked chicken

5 scallions, sliced

¼ cup (31 g) canned water chestnuts, drained and chopped

½ a red bell pepper, diced

6 cups (330 g) chopped lettuce

2 cups (60 g) spinach

½ cup (70 g) roasted, salted cashews

Per serving: 652 calories; 50g fat (68.2% calories from fat); 31g protein; 22g carbohydrate; 6g dietary fiber

Holding the orange half over a bowl, use a sharp knife to cut out the sections. Squeeze the juice left in the rind into the bowl to join what dripped in while you were cutting.

In a jar with a lid, combine the oil, orange juice, rice vinegar, soy sauce, stevia, ginger, garlic, and sherry. Put the lid on and shake it up really well.

Dice up the chicken and put it in a big salad bowl. Pour about half the dressing over it and stir it up. Add the scallions, water chestnuts, and bell pepper and stir again.

Put the lettuce and spinach in your salad bowl. Pour on the remaining dressing and toss like mad.

Pile onto 3 plates. Top each with the chicken mixture. Coarsely chop the cashews, divide between the salads, and serve.

NOTE: All of the prep except for tossing the greens with the dressing and adding the cashews can be done in advance. That way, you can eat this three days in a row instead of sharing it with two other people!

Yield: 3 servings

Curried Chicken Lettuce Wraps

When I created this, I'd done a lot of leafy salads and a lot of cauli-rice salads, and really was looking for something a little different. If you want, you can just pile the lettuce on plates and serve the salad on top, but I find the whole lettuce wrap concept appealing.

1 cup (100 g) pecans

2 cups (280 g) diced cooked chicken

3 celery ribs, finely diced

1 crisp apple, such as a Granny Smith or Gala, diced

3 scallions, thinly sliced

¾ cup (175 g) mayonnaise

2 teaspoons curry powder (hot or mild, as you prefer)

½ a clove of garlic, crushed

10 drops liquid stevia

1 tablespoon (15 ml) white wine vinegar

2 heads of butter lettuce

Per serving: 641 calories; 57g fat (75.8% calories from fat); 26g protein; 15g carbohydrate; 5g dietary fiber

Preheat the oven to 350°F (180°C, or gas mark 4). Spread the pecans on a baking pan and put 'em in the oven. Set the timer for 7 minutes.

In the meanwhile, put the chicken, celery, apple, and scallions in a large bowl.

In a smaller bowl, stir together the mayo, curry powder, garlic, liquid stevia, and vinegar.

Somewhere in here your oven timer will beep. Pull the pecans out, let 'em cool till you can handle them, and chop them to match everything else in size. Throw them into the bowl.

Pour on your dressing and stir it up till everything is well combined.

Core the lettuce but keep the leaves whole. Put a half-head's worth of leaves on each of 4 plates, along with one-quarter of the chicken mixture. Each diner can wrap the salad mixture in the lettuce leaves as he or she goes.

Yield: 4 servings

115

Slaw with Ham and Peanuts

You know how it is with leftover ham. It may take a while to use it up, but you never get tired of how tasty it is. Make this slaw for supper a few days after Easter or take it to work for lunch a few days in a row.

12 cups (840 g) shredded green cabbage or coleslaw mix

¼ cup (40 g) minced red onion

½ cup (115 g) sour cream

½ cup (115 g) mayonnaise

1 tablespoon (15 ml) cider vinegar

1 tablespoon (15 g) brown mustard

16 drops liquid stevia

Salt

2 cups (300 g) cubed ham

½ cup (73 g) chopped dry roasted peanuts

Put the cabbage and onion in a big bowl.

Stir together the sour cream, mayo, vinegar, mustard, and stevia. Pour over the slaw and toss well. Season with salt to taste.

Stir in the ham cubes. Sprinkle the peanuts over each serving.

Yield: 4 servings

Per serving: 545 calories; 46g fat (72.2% calories from fat); 21g protein; 19g carbohydrate; 7g dietary fiber

Ham and Egg Salad

So often ham salad is heavy and gooey. This one is light and crunchy and full of flavor. You'll thank me the Monday after Easter!

¼ cup (28 g) chopped pecans

1 cup (150 g) diced ham

1 cup (120 g) diced celery

¼ cup (40 g) diced red onion

½ cup (75 g) diced green bell pepper

⅓ cup (35 g) sugar-free bread-and-butter pickles, plus 2 tablespoons (28 ml) pickle juice

½ cup (115 g) mayonnaise

1 tablespoon (15 g) brown mustard

3 large hard-boiled eggs

Preheat the oven to 350°F (180°C, or gas mark 4). Spread the pecans on a shallow baking pan, put them in the oven, and set the timer for 7 minutes.

Put the diced ham, celery, onion, bell pepper, and pickles in a bowl.

Somewhere in here the timer will beep. Pull the pecans out of the oven and chop them. Add them to the bowl, too.

Stir together the mayonnaise, mustard, and pickle juice. Add to the salad and stir to coat. Now chop the eggs and stir them in gently, trying to preserve some hunks of yolk. Serve right away if you like, but it's great made ahead, too.

Yield: 3 servings

Per serving: 429 calories; 44g fat (**86.4% calories from fat**); 9g protein; 7g carbohydrate; 2g dietary fiber

Asian Ham Salad

My tester Burma says, "Even my picky hubby loved it!" She also says that at first this didn't seem like enough dressing, but that it turned out to be just right.

½ a head of cauliflower (Trim the very bottom stem.)

1 cup (63 g) snow peas

8 ounces (225 g) ham, cut into small cubes

6 radishes, sliced paper-thin

4 scallions, sliced

3 tablespoons (45 ml) rice vinegar

⅓ cup (80 ml) oil (MCT, sunflower, or light olive)

1 tablespoon (15 ml) dark sesame oil

2 teaspoons soy sauce or coconut aminos

½ a clove of garlic

¼ teaspoon red pepper flakes

¼ cup (35 g) chopped dry-roasted peanuts

Per serving: 512 calories; 43g fat (73.6% calories from fat); 20g protein; 15g carbohydrate; 5g dietary fiber

First, prepare the cauliflower: Cut it into chunks and run it through the shredding blade of your food processor. Put the cauli-rice in a microwaveable casserole with a lid or a microwave steamer and give it 7 minutes on High.

Meanwhile, pinch the ends off the snow peas and pull off any strings. Snip 'em into ½-inch (1.3 cm) bits. When the microwave beeps, open the lid, throw in the pea pod bits, and re-cover. Give the whole thing just another 30 seconds and then uncover to stop the cooking. Let it cool and then dump into a big bowl.

Add the ham, radishes, and scallions.

Put the vinegar, oil, sesame oil, soy sauce, garlic, and red pepper flakes in a blender and run for a few seconds. Pour this over the salad, and toss to mix and coat. Let the whole thing marinate for a while to let the flavors get friendly. You might even chill it for a few hours but bring it back to room temperature to serve.

Pile the salad onto plates and top each serving with chopped peanuts. Serve.

Yield: 3 servings

Leftover-Turkey Salad

You know how you know I'm crazy? I've been known to roast a turkey for just That Nice Boy I Married and me. This makes for a lot of playing with leftovers—and this salad was one simple but great outcome. Dark meat will be higher in fat than light meat, but use what you like.

8 cups (440 g) chopped lettuce

2 scallions, sliced

⅓ cup (80 ml) olive oil

3 tablespoons (45 ml) balsamic vinegar

2 teaspoons brown mustard

1 cup (140 g) diced cooked turkey

1 avocado

Put the lettuce and scallions into a salad bowl.

Put the olive oil, vinegar, and mustard in a jar with a lid and shake like crazy. Pour over the lettuce and toss with abandon until everything's coated. Add the turkey and toss again.

Pile the salad onto 2 plates. Halve, peel, and dice the avocado. Divide between the plates and serve.

Yield: 2 servings

Per serving: 652 calories; 56g fat (74% calories from fat); 26g protein; 18g carbohydrate; 7g dietary fiber

Tex-Mex Pulled Pork Salad

So, you've got a big ol' pot of Tex-Mex Pulled Pork. You're not going to serve it on buns, now are you? What are you going to do with it? Start with this salad. It's great on a hot summer night—and the slow cooker won't heat up the house, either.

¼ of a batch Tex-Mex Pulled Pork (page 151)

1 head of romaine lettuce

½ a batch Mexicali Dressing (page 90)

⅛ of a red onion, sliced paper-thin

1 cup (115 g) shredded Monterey Jack cheese

2 avocados, peeled and diced

½ cup (115 g) sour cream

Salsa, for serving

Tabasco Chipotle sauce, for serving

If the Tex-Mex Pulled Pork is in the fridge, scoop out as much as you'll need and zap it in the microwave for a few minutes to warm it.

Shred the lettuce and throw it in a big ol' salad bowl. Pour on the Mexicali Dressing and toss like a maniac. Pile this onto 4 plates.

Top each with red onion, then a good scoop of Tex-Mex Pulled Pork, a handful of cheese, a whole bunch of diced avocado, and a dollop of sour cream.

Pass the salsa and hot sauce at the table.

Yield: 4 servings

Per serving: 741 calories; 64g fat (75% calories from fat); 30g protein; 18g carbohydrate; 6g dietary fiber

Tex-Mex Turkey Salad or Ensalada de Guatalote

Wondering about the authenticity of the pine nuts here? While most pine nuts we get in our grocery stores are Mediterranean or Chinese pine nuts, pinyon pine nuts are an ancient and important component of New World cuisine. You can serve this on a bed of lettuce, or with big lettuce leaves for wrapping, or stuffed into a tomato, or whatever you like.

¼ cup (34 g) pine nuts

2 cups (280 g) diced cooked turkey

¾ cup (113 g) diced green bell pepper

¾ cup (90 g) diced celery

¼ cup (40 g) diced red onion

2 tablespoons (13 g) chopped black olives

⅔ cup (150 g) Chipotle Mayonnaise (page 45)

¼ cup (4 g) minced fresh cilantro

Per serving: 442 calories; 41g fat (79.2% calories from fat); 19g protein; 5g carbohydrate; 2g dietary fiber

First, put the pine nuts in a dry skillet over medium-low heat and stir until they're turning golden. Remove from the heat.

Put the turkey, bell pepper, celery, onion, and olives in a big bowl.

Stir in the Chipotle Mayonnaise and then the cilantro. Stir in the pine nuts. That's it!

NOTE: If you don't have leftover turkey in the house, you can use deli turkey. Ask the nice deli person to slice it about ½ inch (1.3 cm) thick, and you'll get beautiful cubes.

Yield: 4 servings

Asian Slaw with Grilled Mahi-Mahi

Tester Burma called this "delicious" and says that while any light-flavored oil would work—she used macadamia nut oil—you should only use fresh ginger, not the dried, powdered stuff. She also says to slice the cabbage very thinly, and that if you have the time, you might double the dressing and use half of it to marinate the fish before grilling.

2 teaspoons grated fresh ginger

2 tablespoons (28 g) mayonnaise

1 tablespoon (15 g) brown mustard

12 drops liquid stevia

1 tablespoon (15 ml) soy sauce

½ teaspoon sriracha sauce

3 tablespoons (45 ml) rice vinegar

1 tablespoon (15 ml) lime juice

2 tablespoons (28 ml) dark sesame oil

1 clove of garlic, crushed

¾ cup (175 ml) oil (Use MCT oil or Spectrum expeller-pressed sunflower oil; if you can't get either, use light olive oil.)

1½ pounds (680 g) mahi-mahi steaks (or tuna steaks or any firm fish steaks)

1 head of napa cabbage

1 bunch scallions

1 red bell pepper

¼ cup (4 g) minced fresh cilantro, plus more for garnish (optional)

Salt and ground black pepper

Per serving: 630 calories; 55g fat (77.7% calories from fat); 31g protein; 4g carbohydrate; 1g dietary fiber

Start by putting the ginger, mayo, mustard, stevia, soy sauce, sriracha, vinegar, lime juice, sesame oil, garlic, and oil in your blender or food processor and running it till it's all emulsified.

If it's grilling season, start your grill. If not, you can use a grill pan or even a heavy skillet on the stovetop. Pat the fish dry with paper towels and pour about ¼ cup (60 ml) of the dressing over it, coating both sides. Let that marinate for a few minutes while you continue.

Slice up the cabbage: The easiest way I know is to lay the whole head on the cutting board, cut the head into quarters lengthwise, leaving it connected at the stem, and then cut across the whole thing thinly. Put the cabbage shreds in a big bowl. Slice the scallions and cut the bell pepper into matchstick strips. Add the scallions, bell peppers, and cilantro, if using, to the cabbage.

If you're cooking the fish on the stovetop, put your grill pan or heavy skillet over high heat. Get it good and hot. In the meanwhile, season the fish with salt and pepper.

Put the fish on the grill or in the pan, let it cook for a few minutes, and then flip (the timing will depend on the thickness). Cook the other side until just done through. Transfer to a cutting board and let it sit for a few minutes.

Pour the remaining dressing over the slaw. Toss till everything is well coated. Pile the slaw onto 4 plates. Slice the fish nicely and divide among the plates. A little extra minced cilantro would be pretty on top, but it's not essential.

Yield: 4 servings

Beef

CHAPTER 8

t's funny about beef: We've been told it's terribly fatty, but very few cuts get 70 percent or more of their calories from fat. Often you'll need to add fat, either when cooking the beef itself, or in the form of a sauce, topping, or side dish. This means, of course, that a steak and a big salad with olive oil dressing is the perfect meal. But then, who ever doubted it?

If you can afford grass-fed beef, it is nutritionally superior to the typical grain-finished stuff at the grocery store. Be aware, though, that grass-fed does have a flavor that is distinctly different from that of grain-fed beef; in some cases, it's almost fishy tasting. This comes from the high content of omega-3 fatty acids, so it's good for you, but some people don't enjoy the flavor.

I like it better in some cuts than in others; for instance, I really like a good grass-fed rib-eye but have found that I prefer my grass-fed chuck roast cooked with plenty of seasonings.

It is good to know that Peter Ballerstedt, a Ph.D. forage agronomist (scientist studying the foods that grazing animals eat), points out that even grain-finished cattle are generally grass-fed for most of their lives, eating grains and beans for the last month or six weeks to fatten them. (Yes, the U.S. Department of Agriculture knows that grains and beans make cattle fat. Why they tell us they'll make us thin, I cannot say.) There is a nutritional difference, but nowhere near so great as it would be if the cattle were fed grains and beans all their lives.

The Easiest Tenderized Chuck

Chuck roasts are tough, but if you tenderize them you can then broil, grill, or pan-sear them like any steak—except they're cheaper and more flavorful. Salt is the easiest tenderizer I know.

2 pounds (900 g) beef chuck roast
Kosher salt

Per serving: 315 calories; 24g fat (69% calories from fat); 24g protein; 0g carbohydrate; 0g dietary fiber

This is super-simple. Lay your steak on a cutting board and spread it heavily with coarse kosher salt. No, really, use lots of it, a real crust of it. Don't worry, you'll be rinsing it off later. You don't have to stick holes in it or anything.

Let the chuck stand for at least 1 hour for each inch (2.5 cm) of thickness, and a little longer won't hurt.

When it's done tenderizing, rinse the salt off the chuck. Pat it dry with paper towels. Now cook it as you would any steak: broil, grill, or pan-sear. I pan-sear mine in bacon grease over super-high heat in my big cast-iron skillet. The timing will depend on the thickness of your meat and how well done you like it.

It's always good to let the steak stand for 5 minutes before you cut it into portions and serve. Why not make one of the flavored butters in this book (see page 48 or 49) while you're waiting and melt some over each portion?

NOTES: My chuck roasts are about 1½ inches (3.8 cm) thick. I'm not sure I'd try this with a roast much thicker than that—maybe 2 inches (5 cm), max.

I often use commercial meat tenderizer on chuck steaks, mixed into an acidic marinade—a good balsamic vinaigrette works well. However, it is harder and harder to find meat tenderizer that doesn't have unpleasant additives. This salting method is a great way around that for purists.

Yield: 6 servings

T-Bone with Anchovy Butter and Walnuts

Do you ever get bored of steak? I don't either, but that doesn't mean a little enhancement now and then will be amiss. If you want to use blended steak seasoning, try Montreal seasoning; it's a favorite at my house.

12 ounces (340 g) T-bone steak, ½ inches (3.8 cm) thick

Salt and ground black pepper, or blended steak seasoning

1 tablespoon (14 g) bacon grease or coconut oil

2 tablespoons (15 g) chopped walnuts

⅛ of a batch of Anchovy-Shallot Butter (page 48)

Per serving: 472 calories; 39g fat (75.4% calories from fat); 27g protein; 1g carbohydrate; trace dietary fiber

Put a big, heavy skillet over very high heat. You want it good and hot before you start cooking. Season the steak with salt and pepper on both sides.

When the skillet is hot, add the bacon grease and slosh it around as it melts. Then throw in the steak. Set the timer for 6 minutes.

When the timer beeps, flip the steak and give it another 4 to 5 minutes. Transfer to a platter and let it settle for 5 minutes.

Meanwhile, chop the walnuts, add to the hot skillet, and stir till they smell toasty. Remove from the skillet so they don't burn.

Top each serving of steak with a dollop of the anchovy butter and half the walnuts and serve.

Yield: 2 servings

50/50 Burgers

I heard about this idea of using half beef and half bacon in a burger and had to try it! I added the mushrooms not only to round out the flavor, but also to hold some of the fat that would otherwise melt out. Since I was using grass-fed beef, I hated to lose it!

8 ounces (225 g) bacon

1 cup (70 g) sliced mushrooms

¼ of a small onion

8 ounces (225 g) ground beef

Per serving: 510 calories; 43g fat (77.1% calories from fat); 27g protein; 2g carbohydrate; trace dietary fiber

Snip the bacon into bits about 2 inches (5 cm) long and put it in your food processor, along with the mushrooms and onion. Pulse until it's all ground up. Add the ground beef and pulse until the whole thing is well mixed.

Form into 4 patties about 1 inch (2.5 cm) thick. The mixture will be soft, so it's a nice idea to put them on a plate and refrigerate them for a while to firm them up a little before cooking.

Put your big, heavy skillet over medium-low heat and let it get hot before you throw in the burgers. I can only fit 3 burgers at a time in mine, I'm afraid; you could use another, smaller skillet for the last one if you need to.

(continued on page 124)

50/50 Burgers

(continued from page 123)

Keep the heat fairly low; you don't want them to over-brown before they're done through. I go with 6 to 7 minutes per side on these.

NOTE: I like to melt cheese on these—Cheddar is good, of course, but so is smoked provolone or crumbled blue cheese. Actually, it's hard to think of what cheese wouldn't be good with these.

Yield: 4 servings

Not Your Mama's Meat Loaf

The name of this recipe is courtesy of my tester Laura. The mushrooms not only add a ton of flavor but also help hold fat—especially beneficial if you've paid a pretty price for grass-fed beef.

2 tablespoons (28 g) bacon grease

1 medium onion, chopped

8 ounces (225 g) mushrooms, chopped

1 teaspoon dried thyme

2 teaspoons salt

1 teaspoon ground black pepper

¼ cup (60 ml) chicken broth

2 tablespoons (28 ml) Worcestershire sauce

2 teaspoons tomato paste

1 teaspoon anchovy paste

2½ pounds (1.1 kg) ground beef

½ cup (60 g) pork rind crumbs

2 large eggs

½ cup (120 g) no-sugar-added ketchup

Per serving: 554 calories; 45g fat (73.8% calories from fat); 31g protein; 5g carbohydrate; 1g dietary fiber

Preheat the oven to 325°F (170°C, or gas mark 3).

In your big, heavy skillet over medium heat, melt the bacon grease. Sauté the onions and mushrooms with the thyme until they're soft. Stir in the salt, pepper, chicken broth, Worcestershire sauce, tomato paste, and anchovy paste and cook for a few minutes. Turn off the burner and let it cool till you can handle the mixture.

Put the ground beef in a big bowl. Add the onion-mushroom mix, the pork rind crumbs, and the eggs and use clean hands to squish it all together till well blended.

Form the mixture into a loaf on a baking sheet or the broiler rack, using damp hands to smooth the surface. It should measure about 5 inches (13 cm) wide by 10 inches (25.5 cm) long by 2 inches (5 cm) thick.

Bake for 45 minutes. Spread the ketchup all over the meatloaf and give it another 15 to 25 minutes. Let cool for 10 minutes and serve.

Yield: 8 servings

Bacon-Wrapped Meat Loaf
I mean, what's not to like about bacon-wrapped meat loaf? It's delicious, and it slices beautifully.

⅔ cup (110 g) finely minced onion

4 ounces (115 g) mushrooms, finely chopped

¼ cup (60 ml) olive oil

1½ pounds (680 g) ground beef

1 pound (455 g) ground pork

½ cup (60 g) pork rind crumbs

1 large egg

⅓ cup (80 g) no-sugar-added ketchup

2 teaspoons Worcestershire sauce

1 tablespoon (15 g) brown or Dijon mustard

2 teaspoons salt

¾ teaspoon ground black pepper

¼ cup (15 g) minced fresh parsley

8 bacon slices

Per serving: 576 calories; 48g fat (75.5% calories from fat); 32g protein; 3g carbohydrate; 1g dietary fiber

Preheat the oven to 350°F (180°C, or gas mark 4). Coat your broiler rack with nonstick cooking spray or grease it well.

Put your big, heavy skillet over medium heat, add the oil, and sauté the onions and mushrooms till they're soft. Then let them cool a bit while you put everything else except for the bacon in a big bowl. Using clean hands, start mixing it all together.

When the onions and mushrooms have cooled enough to handle, add them to the meat and squish them in, too. When everything is very well blended, it's time to make the loaf.

Turn the mixture out onto the greased broiler rack, letting it fall in the form of the bowl it's been in. Now squish it a bit more into an oblong loaf measuring 5 to 6 inches (13 to 15 cm) wide, 8 to 9 inches (20 to 23 cm) long, and 2 inches (5 cm) thick.

Working on a diagonal, lay the bacon slices over the loaf, tucking them in at the ends and along the side. Snip off the ends where necessary; surely you can find something else to do with any excess bacon!

Bake for 90 minutes till the bacon is yummy and the juices run clear. Let it stand for 15 minutes before slicing. Spoon the juices from the pan over the slices!

Yield: 8 servings

Pacific Burger

My tester here, who goes by Silvernotes, says, "Even the testers who were skeptical of pineapple on a burger thoroughly enjoyed these. All of them said that the Pacific Burger was a really good blend of flavors." She calls this a quick and delicious meal.

1 pound (455 g) ground beef

Salt and ground black pepper

1 tablespoon (14 g) coconut oil

3 large eggs

¼ cup (60 g) mayonnaise

2 tablespoons (30 g) no-sugar-added ketchup

1 teaspoon sriracha sauce

6 large romaine lettuce leaves

3 tablespoons (45 g) crushed pineapple (fresh, or unsweetened canned)

Per serving: 721 calories; 65g fat **(80.5% calories from fat)**; *31g protein; 4g carbohydrate; trace dietary fiber*

Form the beef into 3 burgers about 1 inch (2.5 cm) thick. At this point, it's nice to refrigerate them for a half an hour or so to firm them up, but it's hardly essential.

When cooking time comes around, season the burgers on both sides with salt and pepper. You can grill the burgers, cook them in your big, heavy skillet over medium-low heat on the stovetop, or even use your electric contact grill, though you'll lose some fat that way. While they're cooking, in a medium-size skillet, melt the coconut oil and put the eggs in to fry.

Stir together the mayonnaise, ketchup, and sriracha sauce.

The burgers and eggs are done! Line each plate with 2 big romaine leaves for wrapping. Layer thusly: burger, sauce, pineapple, egg. Let each diner wrap his or her burger in lettuce and chow down!

NOTE: You may now be stuck with leftover canned pineapple. Freeze it in an ice-cube tray and store in a resealable plastic bag. You'll have pineapple the next time you need it. I do this with tomato paste, too.

Yield: 3 servings

Burgers with Caramelized Onions, Mushrooms, and Bacon

Tester Soren says, "It's fresh, homemade 'fast food' that takes a few minutes to make."

1 pound (455 g) ground beef

6 bacon slices

½ a small red onion, sliced paper-thin

8 ounces (225 g) mushrooms, sliced

1 teaspoon Worcestershire sauce

Salt and ground black pepper

Form your ground beef into 3 patties 1 inch (2.5 cm) thick. Put 'em on a plate and stick 'em in the fridge while you put your big, heavy skillet over medium-low heat. Lay the bacon in it and cook it till it's crisp, turning from time to time. When the bacon is crisp, transfer it from the skillet to a plate, leaving the grease in the skillet.

Add the onions to the skillet and start sautéing them. Cook them till they're limp and starting to brown. Throw the mushrooms into the

(continued on page 127)

Burgers with Caramelized Onions, Mushrooms, and Bacon

(continued from page 126)

Per serving: 572 calories; 47g fat (73.9% calories from fat); 31g protein; 6g carbohydrate; 1g dietary fiber

skillet and keep sautéing until the mushrooms have softened and changed color. Stir in the Worcestershire sauce and turn off the skillet.

Season the burgers with a bit of salt and pepper and then pan-broil, broil, or grill them to your liking.

Top each burger with mushrooms and onions, then 2 slices of bacon —snap the bacon slices in half, so you can crosshatch 'em. Serve!

NOTE: Soren said that a ⅓-pound (150 g) burger seemed small to her. You can jack this up to 1½ pounds (680 g) of ground beef if you want for 8-ounce (225 g) patties, and you'll actually increase the fat percentage to 75 percent. You'll get 43 grams of protein and no additional carbs, of course. I just need to moderate my doses of protein a little; this size burger is about right to me.

Yield: 3 servings

Winter Night Short Ribs
Short ribs are an ideal cut for slow cooking: tough and bony but wildly flavorful. I use grass-fed for extra flavor and nutritional value. They're wonderful.

2 pounds (900 g) beef short ribs

2 tablespoons (28 g) bacon grease

½ a large onion or 1 small one

1 turnip, the size of a baseball

1 cup (235 ml) beef broth

2 tablespoons (32 g) tomato paste

½ teaspoon ground black pepper

½ teaspoon ground cinnamon

¼ teaspoon ground nutmeg

2 cloves of garlic, crushed

Guar or xanthan (optional)

Per serving: 653 calories; 59g fat (82.4% calories from fat); 24g protein; 4g carbohydrate; 1g dietary fiber

In your big, heavy skillet over medium-high heat, sear the short ribs all over in the bacon grease.

While that's happening, slice the onion and peel the turnip and cut it into 1-inch (2.5 cm) cubes. Put these in the bottom of a slow cooker; I use my 4-quart (3.8 L) size.

When the short ribs are brown all over, use tongs to transfer them to the slow cooker, placing them on top of the vegetables.

Pour the broth into the skillet and add everything else. Stir it around over the heat, scraping up any tasty brown bits and making sure everything is well mixed, including any fat in the skillet. Pour this mixture over the ribs, put on the lid, and set to Low. Let it cook for 8 to 9 hours.

You can thicken the broth at the end if you like, but I used good, rich, homemade beef bone broth, and it was great as is. Serve the ribs and vegetables with the liquid from the slow cooker.

Yield: 6 servings

Steak Pinwheels

These pretty pinwheels transform an inexpensive piece of chuck into a dish you'll happily serve to company.

1 pound (455 g) beef chuck, ½ inch (1.3 cm) thick to start with

½ teaspoon meat tenderizer

¼ cup (60 ml) dry red wine

½ cup (120 ml) olive oil

1 clove of garlic, crushed

4 tablespoons (55 g) butter, softened

2 tablespoons (30 g) pesto sauce

¼ cup (28 g) oil-packed sun-dried tomatoes

3 tablespoons (15 g) grated Parmesan cheese

4 ounces (115 g) fresh spinach

Per serving: 531 calories; 50g fat
(84.4% calories from fat); 18g protein;
3g carbohydrate; 1g dietary fiber

Sprinkle both sides of the beef with the tenderizer. Pierce it all over with a fork.

Mix together the wine, olive oil, and garlic. Put the chuck in a 1-gallon (3.8 L) resealable plastic bag. Pour the mixture over it, press out the air, and seal the bag. Now, turn it a few times to coat. Let the steak marinate for 20 to 30 minutes. Turn it once during that time if you think of it.

While the steak is marinating, put the butter and pesto through your food processor until they're well combined.

Pour off the marinade into a small dish and reserve. Reseal the bag and use the nearest heavy blunt object to pound the steak all over until it's maybe ⅓ inch (8 mm) thick.

Take the steak out of the bag and lay it on a cutting board. Use a rubber scraper to spread the pesto butter evenly over the whole surface of the steak.

Put the sun-dried tomatoes in the food processor bowl—no need to clean the residue of the pesto butter out of it—and pulse until they're chopped to a coarse paste. Spread this over the pesto butter. Sprinkle the Parmesan evenly over the tomatoes. Now cover the whole surface of the thing with spinach leaves.

Starting with one of the narrow ends, roll the whole thing up. Stick toothpicks in the roll about 2 inches (5 cm) apart to keep it from unrolling. Now use a sharp, straight-bladed knife to slice between the toothpicks, making pretty pinwheel-like rolls. Arrange these down the middle of your broiler rack. (The ones from the ends will not be as picturesque as the ones from the middle. That's just the way it goes.)

Put the oven shelf about 6 inches (15 cm) under the broiler and preheat the broiler. Baste the top of the pinwheels with the reserved

(continued on page 129)

Steak Pinwheels
(continued from page 128)

marinade and slide the rack under the heat. Give them about 7 minutes, depending on your preferred degree of doneness.

Pull out the broiler rack, carefully flip the pinwheels, and baste again with the marinade. Pour the rest down the sink; the heat will be killing the germs on the pinwheels, but you don't want to use the marinade unheated. Turn the broiler rack end-to-end, to help with even cooking, and slide it back in. Mine only took about another 4 minutes, but again, go with your doneness preference. Carefully transfer to plates and serve.

Yield: 5 servings

Where There's Smoke There's Fire Chili
To get the 70 percent fat percentage on this chili, I added bacon and subbed mushrooms for the usual beans. The mushrooms absorb the bacon grease and beef fat and add flavor without being obviously mushroom-y.

4 bacon slices

1 pound (455 g) ground beef

1 cup (70 g) chopped mushrooms

½ an onion, chopped

10 ounces (280 g) canned tomatoes with green chiles

2 tablespoons (30 g) no-sugar-added ketchup

2 tablespoons (12 g) unsweetened cocoa powder

2 tablespoons (15 g) chili powder

1 tablespoon (7 g) smoked paprika

2 teaspoons dried oregano

½ cup (235 ml) water

1 teaspoon beef bouillon concentrate

Start by putting your big, heavy skillet over medium heat and frying the bacon crisp. Remove it from the skillet, put it on a plate, and let it hang out while you put the ground beef in the skillet and start browning and crumbling it. After a couple of minutes, add the mushrooms and onion.

When the beef is all browned, add everything else and stir it all up well. Turn the burner to low and let the chili simmer for 20 minutes or so.

Crumble the bacon and top each serving with some. I like to add diced avocado, shredded Cheddar, and sour cream to my chili, for an even higher fat percentage.

Yield: 5 servings

Per serving: 351 calories; 28g fat (70% calories from fat); 19g protein; 8g carbohydrate; 3g dietary fiber

Creamy Beef Skillet Supper

I make this with a pound (455 g) of leftover chuck from The Easiest Tenderized Chuck on page 122, but you could start from scratch and brown slightly over a pound (455 g) of ground chuck to use instead.

½ a head of cauliflower (Trim the very bottom stem.)

8 ounces (225 g) mushrooms, sliced

¼ of a medium onion, diced

3 tablespoons (42 g) butter

1½ cups (186 g) frozen green beans—cross-cut, thawed

1 pound (455 g) cooked beef chuck (leftover steak, or ground chuck browned fresh)

2 teaspoons beef bouillon concentrate

2 tablespoons (28 ml) Worcestershire sauce

½ cup (60 ml) heavy cream

3 ounces (85 g) cream cheese

Salt and ground black pepper

Per serving: 438 calories; 36g fat (73.1% calories from fat); 19g protein; 11g carbohydrate; 3g dietary fiber

Cut the cauliflower into ½-inch (1.3 cm) chunks and put it in a microwaveable casserole dish with a lid or a microwaveable steamer. Add a few tablespoons (45 to 60 ml) water, cover, and nuke on High for about 10 minutes until tender but not mushy.

In the meanwhile, put your big, heavy skillet over medium-low heat and start sautéing the mushrooms and onion in the butter.

When the microwave beeps, take the cauliflower out and uncover it immediately to stop the cooking. In the meanwhile, put the green beans in a smaller bowl, add just a tablespoon (15 ml) of water, and cover. Nuke this for 4 minutes or until tender-crisp. (The easiest way I know to cover a small bowl for the microwave is to set a saucer on top.)

While the beans are cooking, cut your leftover beef into bite-size strips.

By now, the mushrooms should have softened and changed color and the onions turned translucent. Add the cauliflower, beans, and beef to the skillet, and stir it all up.

Stir the bouillon and Worcestershire sauce into the cream and pour it into the skillet. Cut the cream cheese into small chunks and put them on top of the whole thing. Cover the skillet and turn the burner to the lowest heat. Let it cook for 5 minutes or so.

Stir the melted cream cheese in till you have a creamy sauce. Season with salt and pepper to taste and serve in bowls.

NOTE: If you're using ground chuck, start browning and crumbling it first. When a little fat cooks out of it, add the butter, mushrooms, and onion and proceed from there.

Yield: 5 servings

South of the Border Leftover Steak Supper

If you tenderize a chuck roast to grill or broil, chances are you'll have leftovers. Here's how to turn them into the next night's supper.

3 tablespoons (42 g) coconut oil or lard

½ cup (80 g) diced onion

½ cup (75 g) diced green bell pepper, or red, or mixed

1 tablespoon (9 g) minced jalapeño chile (optional)

4 cloves of garlic, crushed

2 teaspoons ground cumin

2 tablespoons (28 ml) hot sauce (I like Tabasco Chipotle.)

6 large eggs

8 ounces (225 g) cooked beef chuck, cut into small cubes or strips

2 avocados

Salt and ground black pepper

¼ cup (4 g) minced fresh cilantro (optional)

Per serving: 489 calories; 41g fat (74% calories from fat); 20g protein; 13g carbohydrate; 4g dietary fiber

Put your big, heavy skillet over medium-low heat, melt the coconut oil or lard, and start sautéing the vegetables. When the onion is turning translucent, stir in the garlic, cumin, and hot sauce.

Scramble up the eggs with a whisk and have them ready by the stove.

Add the beef bits to the skillet and stir till they're warm through. Now pour in the eggs and scramble till they're set. Dish up on 4 plates.

Slice the avocados and divide the slices on top of each serving. Season lightly with salt and pepper, add cilantro if you like it, and serve. Pass the hot sauce for those who want more.

NOTE: Feel free to use 8 ounces (225 g) of ground chuck if you don't have leftover beef.

Yield: 4 servings

Poultry

CHAPTER 9

Most poultry runs below our 70 percent fat target. This means, among other things, that rather than feeling guilty about eating the yummy, crispy skin on your chicken, you can feel guilty for *not* eating it. You can also, if you like, indulge in one of my private pleasures: eating crusty brown chicken drippings right out of the roasting pan. It's heaven.

As every dieter in the country knows, the boneless, skinless chicken breast is the lowest-fat cut of chicken available. I have always found them bland and boring unless carefully doctored; I much prefer dark meat. Thanks to all those folks who will only eat boneless, skinless breast (or "tenders"), I've been getting legs and thighs on the cheap for years. I suggest you do the same.

Boneless, skinless breast gets 21 percent of its calories from fat. It takes a lot of sauce to overcome numbers like that. Skinless thigh gets 31 percent of its calories from fat. Eat the skin with that thigh, and you jump to 67 percent of calories from fat. (That's before cooking. Some of that fat cooks out.) A nice roasted chicken thigh with a big salad or some broccoli with lemon butter, and you're right about where you need to be.

The point is, unless you really dislike it, choose dark meat over white when you're keeping your fat intake high.

Or just eat duck. There's only one duck recipe in this chapter, because I know I can't afford it all the time, and I expect you can't, either. But boy, it's fatty—89 percent before cooking—and it sure is delicious. Plus, the fat that cooks out of a roasting duck is pure culinary gold.

Super-Crunchy Chicken! I was looking for something to please all you folks who miss the crunch of fried chicken. This works beautifully!

1 large egg

2 teaspoons water

1 tablespoon (15 g) brown mustard

2 drops liquid stevia

½ cup (50 g) grated Parmesan or romano cheese, or a blend of the two

½ cup (60 g) pork rind crumbs

½ teaspoon salt

¼ teaspoon ground black pepper

4 bone-in, skin-on chicken thighs

5 tablespoons (70 g) butter, cut into pieces

Per serving: 449 calories; 36g fat (73.5% calories from fat); 29g protein; 1g carbohydrate; 0g dietary fiber

Preheat the oven to 350°F (180°C, or gas mark 4). If you hate dishwashing, line an 8-inch (20 cm) square pan with aluminum foil. (If the thighs are really big, you may need a bigger one.)

On a rimmed plate, combine the egg, water, mustard, and liquid stevia. Mix 'em up with a fork until you have no big globs of white, but rather a fairly even texture. On another plate, combine the Parmesan cheese, pork pind crumbs, salt, and pepper.

One by one, roll the chicken in the egg, then in the crumb-cheese mixture, covering the entire surface. Arrange the chicken in the pan.

Dot the chicken with half the butter. Stick it in the oven and set a timer for 30 minutes.

Take the chicken out, dot it with the rest of the butter and put it back in. Let it roast for another 15 minutes or so.

Serve! (And enjoy picking little bits of crunchy stuff out of the pan.)

Yield: 4 servings

Creamy Sage and Parmesan Chicken This isn't authentically anything, but it strikes me as kind of Northern Italian. It's divine. You'll want shirataki, Zoodles (page 95), or cauli-rice to soak up the sauce.

¼ cup (60 ml) olive oil

4 skin-on, bone-in chicken thighs

1 shallot, minced

4 cloves of garlic, crushed

½ cup (120 ml) chicken broth

¼ cup (60 ml) dry white wine

1 tablespoon (2 g) dried sage

¼ cup (60 ml) heavy cream

¼ cup (25 g) grated Parmesan cheese

¼ teaspoon ground black pepper

In your big, heavy skillet over medium heat, heat the olive oil and brown the chicken all over. Get it beautifully golden.

When the chicken is browned, transfer to a plate and pour off about half the fat in the pan, leaving about ¼ cup (60 ml) of fat in the pan. Save the rest of the mixture of olive oil and chicken fat for cooking.

Put the skillet back on the burner and throw in the shallot. Sauté it for just a minute. Add the garlic, chicken broth, wine, and sage, and stir it around. Now put the chicken back in the skillet, cover it, and turn the burner to low. Set your timer for 20 minutes.

(continued on page 134)

Creamy Sage and Parmesan Chicken

(continued from page 133)

Per serving: 415 calories; 35g fat (78.1% calories from fat); 20g protein; 3g carbohydrate; trace dietary fiber

When the timer beeps, pierce the largest piece of chicken to the bone to test for doneness. If the juices run clear, it's done; if they run pink, give it another 5 minutes or so.

Transfer the chicken to a plate, turn up the heat, and let the liquid in the skillet reduce by at least half; you want it to be getting a little syrupy.

Whisk in the cream, then the Parmesan and pepper. Let it cook for just another minute and then serve the chicken with the sauce.

Yield: 4 servings

Quasi-French Chicken
Chicken in a rich, creamy, succulent "pink sauce" (made with tomatoes and sour cream) is another great opportunity for cauli-rice!

---

6 bone-in, skin-on chicken thighs (about 3 pounds, or 1.4 kg)
Salt and ground black pepper
2 tablespoons (28 g) butter
2 tablespoons (28 ml) olive oil
½ cup (80 g) chopped onion
1 medium carrot, shredded
1 cup (180 g) canned diced tomatoes
½ cup (120 ml) dry white wine
½ cup (120 ml) chicken broth
2 teaspoons tomato paste
1 tablespoon (5 g) dried tarragon
½ cup (115 g) sour cream

Per serving: 355 calories; 27g fat (70.8% calories from fat); 18g protein; 7g carbohydrate; 1g dietary fiber

While your big, heavy skillet is heating over medium-high heat, season the chicken with salt and pepper on both sides.

In the skillet, melt the butter with the olive oil and swirl them together. Now add the chicken, skin side down, and let it cook till the skin is browned. Flip it and let the bottom brown a little, too.

When the chicken is nicely browned, use tongs to transfer it to a plate. Add the onion and carrot to the fat in the skillet and let them sauté for 5 minutes or so.

Add the canned tomatoes, wine, chicken broth, tomato paste, and tarragon and stir it all up. Place the chicken back in the skillet, skin side up, nestling it down in the sauce.

Cover the skillet with a tilted lid (that is, leave a crack for steam to escape) and turn the burner to low. Let it simmer for 30 minutes or so.

Using tongs, transfer the chicken to a plate and keep it warm. Use your stick blender to partially blend up the vegetables in the skillet—you can puree them entirely if you like, but I find the sauce more interesting with some texture.

Whisk in the sour cream, heat through, and serve the chicken with the sauce.

Yield: 6 servings

Pollo en Mole de Cacahuates
It's Mexican peanut sauce! What's not to love about that?

5 chicken legs (leg and thigh quarters)

2 tablespoons (28 ml) olive oil, or (28 g) lard, if you can get the good stuff

3 cups (700 ml) chicken broth

2 teaspoons pure ground chile powder, such as ancho

½ teaspoon ground black pepper

1 teaspoon ground allspice

½ teaspoon ground cinnamon

¼ teaspoon ground cloves

1 can (14 ounces, or 390 g) diced tomatoes

2 canned chipotle chiles in adobo sauce, plus 2 to 3 tablespoons (28 to 45 g) of the adobo sauce

1 teaspoon guar or xanthan

1½ cups (220 g) dry-roasted peanuts, divided

½ a medium onion, chopped

2 cloves of garlic, crushed

Per serving: 556 calories; 40g fat **(64% calories from fat)***; 38g protein; 14g carbohydrate; 5g dietary fiber*

Strip the skin off the chicken, saving it to make Chicken Chips (page 41). (You could start with skinless chicken, if you like, but it's hard to find skinless legs and thighs with the bones, and this is best cooked on the bone. And anyway, you'll miss the chance to make Chicken Chips!) Cut the legs and thighs apart at the joint.

Put your biggest, heaviest skillet over medium-high heat and add the olive oil or lard. When the fat is hot, add the chicken (you may need to do this in a couple of batches) and start browning it. You just want a little gold on both sides.

While that's happening, throw the chicken broth, chile powder, pepper, allspice, cinnamon, cloves, tomatoes, chipotles, adobo sauce, guar, and 1 cup (145 g) of the peanuts into a blender. Cover it and turn it on. Go turn the chicken!

As the chicken is browned, use tongs to transfer it to a large slow cooker. When all the chicken is browned and in the cooker, turn the heat under the skillet down to medium-low and throw in the chopped onion, adding a little more fat if needed.

When the onion is soft and translucent, add the garlic and sauté everything for just another minute. Scrape this mixture into the blender and blend that in, too. The sauce should be smooth, not chunky.

Pour the sauce over the chicken, cover the pot, and set it to Low. Let it cook for 6 to 8 hours.

Just before serving, chop the remaining peanuts. Serve the chicken and sauce with a sprinkle of chopped peanuts over each serving.

Yield: 6 servings

Jalapeño-Lime Stuffed Chicken

I really don't recommend boneless, skinless chicken breast on a low-carb, high-fat diet; you have to add a lot of fat! This is a really, really great way to do that, however.

8 ounces (225 g) cream cheese, softened

4 teaspoons (20 ml) lime juice

½ a jalapeño chile, finely diced

2 scallions, sliced

2 tablespoons (2 g) minced fresh cilantro

1 clove of garlic, crushed

1½ pounds (680 g) chicken breast (about 2 large ones)

3 tablespoons (42 g) butter

1 batch pork rind crumbs

1 teaspoon ground cumin

Per serving: 631 calories; 48g fat (68.6% calories from fat); 46g protein; 3g carbohydrate; trace dietary fiber

Preheat the oven to 375°F (190°C, or gas mark 5). Grease a baking pan or coat with nonstick cooking spray.

Put the cream cheese, lime juice, jalapeño, scallions, cilantro, and garlic in your food processor and run till it's all mixed up but the jalapeño and scallion aren't completely pulverized. (Don't forget to wash your hands thoroughly after handling that jalapeño!)

Now it's time to beat the chicken breasts into submission: Put one in a big resealable plastic bag, press out the air, and seal it. Now grab the nearest blunt, heavy object. Whack that sucker with controlled ferocity (you don't want to make holes in it, after all) until it's beaten to an even ½-inch (1.3 cm) thickness. Repeat with the second chicken breast.

Lay one of your chicken breasts on your cutting board, rough side (the bottom side) up. Use a rubber scraper to spread half the cheese mixture evenly over the entire surface. Roll it up. Repeat with the second breast and the rest of the cheese mixture. Cut each roll into 2 portions.

Put the butter on a rimmed plate and nuke it for a minute to melt. While that's happening, mix the pork rind crumbs with the cumin. Roll each chicken-cheese bundle in the butter, then in the crumbs, coating entirely. Arrange in the baking pan.

Bake for 40 to 45 minutes, until the juices run clear and the chicken feels done—you know, kinda firm when pressed and crispy on the outside. Serve!

Yield: 4 servings

Chicken Lo Mein

Okay, Japanese noodles aren't authentic in lo mein, but they work very well here. This stir-fry comes together very quickly, so make sure you do all your prep work before you begin cooking.

1 package tofu shirataki, fettuccine-style

10 ounces (280 g) skinless chicken thighs

1 cup (75 g) sliced Chinese cabbage

½ cup (50 g) sliced celery

4 scallions, cut into ½-inch (1.3 cm) pieces long

1 cup (52 g) mung bean sprouts

2 tablespoons (28 ml) soy sauce

1 tablespoon (15 ml) dry sherry

1 tablespoon grated fresh ginger

1 clove of garlic, crushed

2 to 4 drops liquid stevia

¼ cup (56 g) coconut oil

Per serving: 385 calories; 32g fat (72.8% calories from fat); 14g protein; 13g carbohydrate; 5g dietary fiber

Snip open the packet of shirataki and dump them into a strainer (over the sink, of course). Rinse them well. Now use your kitchen shears to snip across them in a few different directions 'cause in their natural state they're too darned long.

Cut the chicken thighs into ½-inch (1.3 cm) cubes. Put on a plate next to the stove.

Slice the Chinese cabbage across the whole head, about ¼ inch (6 mm) thick. Slice the celery quite thin. Cut the scallions into ½-inch (1.3 cm) lengths. Put all this, along with the bean sprouts, on a bigger plate, and set it by the stove, too.

In a small dish, combine the soy sauce, sherry, ginger root, garlic, and stevia. Stir it up. Set this by the stove as well.

Put your wok or a big skillet over the highest heat. When it's good and hot, add half the oil, let it melt, and throw in the chicken. Stir-fry it until all the pink is gone. Scoop it out of the wok and onto a clean plate.

Put the rest of the oil in the skillet, let it melt, and dump in the vegetables. Stir-fry for just a minute or two—all of these are vegetables that cook quickly.

When the veggies are just barely getting tender, throw the chicken back in the wok and add the soy sauce mixture. Stir it all up. Turn the burner down to medium-low.

Stir in the shirataki, let the whole thing simmer for just a minute or so more, and then serve.

Yield: 2 servings

Chicken Livers with Mushrooms and Artichokes

Can we lay to rest the old canard about the liver being "the filter of the body?" It is not; it is the processing plant of the body, and I know of nothing more nutritious. I adore chicken livers, and this is an amazingly great way to cook them. Want to make it even more filling? Put a couple of fried eggs on top. Wow.

Mushroom and Artichoke Sauté (page 105)

12 chicken livers, patted dry and cut into bite-size chunks

Salt and ground black pepper

Per serving: 352 calories; 22g fat (58.4% calories from fat); 21g protein; 14g carbohydrate; 1g dietary fiber

Leave the oil in the pan from making the Mushroom and Artichoke Sauté (or if you made it ahead, reserve the oil and reheat it).

Throw the chicken liver bits into the oil left in the pan and sauté till the surfaces have changed color and the juices are running pink, but not bright red. Do not overcook! Sprinkle with salt and pepper while cooking.

When the livers are just done, divide them between the plates. Serve.

Yield: 4 servings

Sautéed Chicken Livers with Mushrooms

This is quite filling as is, but feel free to add another few chicken livers if you want even more protein.

8 chicken livers

⅔ cup (150 g) coconut oil

1 pound (455 g) mushrooms, sliced

4 small celery ribs, sliced (You could use a couple of big ones, but the little ones are more tender.)

½ cup (80 g) minced shallot

½ cup (55 g) oil-packed sun-dried tomatoes, minced

¼ cup (15 g) minced fresh parsley

1 tablespoon (15 ml) Worcestershire sauce

Salt and ground black pepper

Per serving: 475 calories; 41g fat (74.6% calories from fat); 15g protein; 16g carbohydrate; 3g dietary fiber

With kitchen shears, cut the chicken livers into bite-size chunks.

Put your big, heavy skillet over medium-high heat. Melt a good ⅓ cup (75 g) of the oil.

Throw in the mushrooms, celery, and shallot and sauté till the mushrooms have softened and changed color and the celery is tender-crisp. Scoop the mixture out and pile it on a plate. Put the skillet back over the heat.

Melt the rest of the fat. Add the chicken livers and sauté quickly until the surfaces have "seized"—changed color and the juice is no longer running red. Do not overcook!

Quickly add the vegetables back to the skillet, along with the sun-dried tomatoes and parsley, and stir it all up. Add the Worcestershire sauce and stir. Season with salt and pepper to taste and serve.

Yield: 4 servings

Thanksgiving Weekend Curry
This curry is amazing, if I do say so myself. If you don't have any leftover turkey in the house, you could cut up a rotisserie chicken instead.

½ a medium onion, chopped

4 cups (560 g) diced cooked turkey

3 tablespoons (42 g) coconut oil

2 teaspoons garam masala

1 teaspoon ground cinnamon

1 teaspoon ground turmeric

1¾ cups (410 ml) coconut milk

¾ cup (175 ml) chicken broth, or turkey broth if you have it

2 cloves of garlic, crushed

1 tablespoon (8 g) grated fresh ginger

1 teaspoon cayenne pepper

Salt

Per serving: 349 calories; 27g fat (69.1% calories from fat); 23g protein; 4g carbohydrate; 1g dietary fiber

Start by chopping the onion and dicing the turkey, so you have them on hand.

In your big, heavy skillet, over medium-low heat, melt the oil. Add the garam masala, cinnamon, and turmeric and stir for a minute or so.

Add the onion and sauté until it's translucent.

Now add the coconut milk, chicken broth, garlic, ginger, and cayenne. Stir it up until you've got a creamy sauce.

Stir in the turkey and turn the burner to low. Let the whole thing simmer for 15 minutes or so.

Season with salt to taste and serve. You can serve this over cauli-rice or shirataki, if you like, but we like to just eat it from bowls with soup spoons.

Yield: 6 servings

139

About Turkey

Chances are good that you only roast a turkey once or twice a year, on holidays, but I encourage you to think of turkey whenever you have a gang to feed. Consider the virtues: It's cheap, it's easy (it takes a while, but it's very little work), it's widely available, everybody but vegetarians likes it, and as far as I know it doesn't violate any religious restrictions. Slow-smoked on the grill, it even makes great cookout food. Plus, you'll likely have leftovers to play with!

Since I have more freezer space than anyone but a grocer really needs (I have three-count-'em-three freezers, including a 23-cubic-foot chest freezer), I grab a couple of extra turkeys after the holidays, when they drop to 70 cents per pound. Thawing time means these aren't spontaneous, but with a couple of days notice, I'm always ready to feed a crowd.

And being not entirely sane, I've been known to roast a smallish turkey for just my husband and me. What can I say? We like turkey!

Creamy Turkey Casserole

You know how it is after Thanksgiving—two days later you're out of stuffing and gravy, but you still have plenty of turkey to use up. Here's how!

- 4 cups (400 g) cauliflower, cut in ½-inch (1.3 cm) chunks
- 10 bacon slices, cooked
- 4 ounces (115 g) cream cheese
- ½ cup (120 ml) heavy cream
- 2 tablespoons (30 g) brown mustard
- 1 tablespoon (15 ml) cider vinegar
- Salt and ground black pepper
- 2 cups (280 g) diced cooked turkey
- ½ cup (55 g) oil-packed sun-dried tomatoes, chopped
- 1 bunch scallions, sliced
- ¼ cup (25 g) grated Parmesan cheese

Per serving: 391 calories; 30g fat (67.8% calories from fat); 23g protein; 9g carbohydrate; 3g dietary fiber

Preheat the oven to 350°F (180°C, or gas mark 4). Grease a 3-quart (2.8 L) microwaveable casserole dish or coat with nonstick cooking spray.

Put the cauliflower in the casserole. Add a couple of tablespoons (28 ml) of water, cover, and nuke on High for 8 minutes (you're par-cooking it).

Melt the cream cheese into the heavy cream and whisk in the mustard and vinegar. Season with salt and pepper to taste.

Okay, it's assembly time: Drain the cauliflower and put it back in the casserole. Add the turkey, tomatoes, and scallions and stir them in. Crumble in half the bacon and stir that in, too. Pour the sauce over the whole thing.

Sprinkle the Parmesan on top. Bake for 30 minutes until the sauce is bubbly and the top is golden.

Crumble the rest of the bacon over the top and serve.

NOTE: If you'd like to make this without roasting a turkey, you can make this recipe with deli turkey breast. Ask the deli folks to slice it ½-inch (1.3 cm) thick, and it'll be a snap to cut it into cubes.

Yield: 5 servings

Seared Duck Breasts with Raspberry-Chipotle Sauce

This makes a wonderful quick romantic dinner. Try it for Valentine's Day. Personally, I think steamed asparagus would be a really nice side dish here, maybe with some hollandaise, and a Pinot Noir to drink, but it's your menu.

2 boneless, skin-on duck breasts, 6 ounces (170 g) each

Salt and ground black pepper

1 tablespoon (14 g) butter

1 tablespoon (15 ml) olive oil

1 tablespoon (10 g) minced onion

1 tablespoon (8 g) minced canned chipotle chile in adobo sauce

¼ cup (80 g) low-sugar raspberry preserves

1 tablespoon (15 ml) balsamic vinegar

Per serving: 652 calories; 61g fat (84.1% calories from fat); 14g protein; 11g carbohydrate; trace dietary fiber; 11g usable carb.

Use a sharp, straight-bladed knife to score the skin on the duck breasts, about 1 inch (2.5 cm) apart, into squares or diamonds. Cut through the skin but not into the meat. Season with salt and pepper and let them sit for 10 minutes.

Preheat the oven to 300°F (150°C, or gas mark 2). Have a small baking pan standing by.

Put your big, heavy skillet over medium-high heat. Add the butter and olive oil and swirl them together as the butter melts. Let the pan get thoroughly hot.

Lay the duck breasts skin side down in the skillet. Let them cook until the skin is brown and crisp, somewhere between 5 and 10 minutes. Flip the breasts and let them continue cooking until the juices are no longer running red, but are still a bit pink. Transfer the duck to the baking pan and put in the oven to stay warm.

Pour off about half the fat in the skillet, which will now include duck fat as well as butter and olive oil. Don't discard this! Save for cooking; it's delicious. Put the pan back over the heat, and turn the burner down to medium. Throw in the onion and sauté for a minute or two until it's turning translucent. Stir in everything else, whisking till smooth. Let it cook for another minute, till syrupy. Turn the heat off.

Slice the duck breasts on the bias and arrange on 2 plates. Top with the sauce, dividing it between them, and serve immediately.

Yield: 2 servings

Pork and Lamb

Along with teaching everyone in the world to make an omelet, I am making it my life's purpose (okay, one of my life's purposes) to redeem the good name of pork. Likely because of various religious proscriptions against it, many people think of pork as less healthful than other flesh foods, such as chicken, turkey, fish, or even beef.

That is stuff and nonsense. Pork is not only a fine protein source, but it is also an excellent source of zinc, thiamin, niacin, and riboflavin, and a remarkably good source of potassium. As for trichinosis, it's virtually unheard of in modern pork; the few cases that still happen come from wild game.

Sadly, the low-fat fad of the past few decades has resulted in the breeding of much leaner hogs. However, it has also led to the fattier cuts like shoulder—aka picnic or Boston butt roast —becoming remarkably cheap. We can take advantage of this price differential.

If you can find pork from heritage breed hogs, allowed to run in a pasture, snap it up. It's better for you, better for the environment, and better for the hogs. And the bacon I get from local small farms is truly the food of the gods.

As for lamb, I cannot for the life of me figure out why Americans don't eat more of it. I grew up on it, and I love the stuff. Furthermore, pretty much all the lamb we get is grass-fed, making it nutritionally superior to a lot of beef. C'mon, try a lamb burger.

Amazing Mediterranean Pork Steak
This is one of those "Hmmm. What do I have on hand?" recipes, and it's fabulous, if I do say so myself. I'd be happy to pay for this at an upscale restaurant.

- 12 ounces (340 g) pork shoulder steak, ½ inch (1.3 cm) thick
- 2 tablespoons (28 ml) olive oil, divided
- 1 small green bell pepper
- ¼ of a small onion, diced
- 6 green olives, pitted and sliced
- 2 teaspoons capers, drained and chopped
- 1 tablespoon (15 ml) dry white wine
- 2 tablespoons (28 ml) chicken broth
- ¼ cup (60 ml) heavy cream
- 1 teaspoon tomato paste
- ¼ teaspoon red pepper flakes
- Salt and ground black pepper

Per serving: 561 calories; 49g fat (79.3% calories from fat); 23g protein; 5g carbohydrate; 1g dietary fiber

In your big, heavy skillet over medium-high heat, sear your pork steak a bit on both sides in 1 tablespoon (15 ml) of the olive oil. Remove it from the pan.

Add the rest of the olive oil to the pan and throw in the bell pepper, onion, sliced olives, and chopped capers. Stir them around, sautéing them for a minute.

Add the white wine and chicken broth and stir it all around, scraping up the browned bits from the bottom of the skillet. Now put the steak back in the pan, spooning some of the liquid over it. Turn the heat to low, cover, and let the whole thing simmer for 20 minutes.

Transfer the steak to a plate and keep it warm. Turn up the heat to medium. Let the wine and broth reduce by about half.

Whisk in the cream, tomato paste, and red pepper flakes. Let the sauce cook for another minute or two.

Season the sauce with salt and pepper to taste, spoon it all over the steak, and bear it forth, rejoicing.

Yield: 2 servings

143

Pork with Sage, Parmesan, and Browned Butter Very Italian.

12 ounces (308 g) pork shoulder steak

Salt and ground black pepper

1 tablespoon (15 ml) olive oil

3 tablespoons (15 g) grated Parmesan cheese

1 tablespoon (3 g) fresh sage leaves, chopped

3 tablespoons (42 g) butter

Per serving: 365 calories; 31g fat **(81% calories from fat)**; *17g protein; trace carbohydrate, 0g dietary fiber*

Put your big, heavy skillet over medium heat. Sprinkle the pork steaks on both sides with salt and pepper. Heat the olive oil in the skillet and then sauté the pork steaks till they're brown on both sides and done through; how long will depend on how thick they are.

Cut the steaks into portions and divide among 3 plates. Top each with Parmesan and sage, spreading it as evenly as possible. Keep them warm.

Melt the butter in the skillet. Let it get bubbling hot, even beginning to brown. Pour it over the pork steaks and serve immediately.

Yield: 3 servings

Sausage-y Spareribs Now it's time for some things to do with spareribs other than slow-smoke them. I love slow-smoked ribs as much as the next girl, but not enough to fire up the grill when there's snow on the ground. Guess what? You can do other things with ribs.

2 pounds (900 g) pork spareribs (half a slab)

1 tablespoon (14 g) coconut oil or lard, melted

1½ teaspoons dried thyme

1½ teaspoons ground dried sage

1 teaspoon ground black pepper

½ teaspoon dried rosemary

2 tablespoons (30 g) no-sugar-added ketchup

1 tablespoon (20 g) sugar-free pancake syrup

1 tablespoon (15 ml) sriracha sauce

Per serving: 440 calories; 37g fat (76.2% calories from fat); 24g protein; 2g carbohydrate, 0g dietary fiber

Preheat the oven to 300°F (150°C, or gas mark 2).

Lay the ribs in a roasting pan. Brush all over with the melted oil or lard.

Mix together the thyme, sage, pepper, and rosemary. Sprinkle all over the ribs, covering both sides.

Roast the ribs for a good 3 hours, flipping them and basting them with the fat in the pan every 30 minutes or so.

When they're getting tender and the meat is starting to pull away from the bone, mix together the ketchup, pancake syrup, and sriracha. Brush all over the ribs.

Give 'em another 10 minutes in the oven, and serve.

Yield: 4 servings

Braised Spareribs

Have you only had spareribs barbecued? You don't know what you're missing. This would be a great time to serve Mixed Mash fauxtatoes (page 95), to soak up more of the savory pot juices.

4 bacon slices

2 pounds (900 g) pork spareribs (half a slab)

Salt and ground black pepper

8 ounces (225 g) portobello mushrooms, sliced

2 shallots, minced

1 cup (235 ml) chicken broth

½ cup (120 ml) Marsala

2 teaspoons dried thyme

1½ teaspoons dried rosemary

Guar or xanthan (optional)

Per serving: 489 calories; 37g Fat (71.5% calories from fat); 29g protein; 5g carbohydrate; 1g dietary fiber

Put your Dutch oven over medium-low heat, and lay the bacon in it. Cook till crisp and then transfer to a plate and reserve.

Cut your spareribs into lengths that will fit in the Dutch oven, and season them with a bit of salt and pepper. When the bacon is done and out of there, turn up the heat to medium-high, throw in the spareribs, and brown them all over. Remove them from the pot, too—might as well let them howdy with the bacon.

Throw in the sliced mushrooms and shallots. Sauté them together until they've softened.

Put the spareribs back into the Dutch oven. Mix together the chicken broth, Marsala, thyme, and rosemary. Pour this mixture over the ribs and vegetables. Crumble in the bacon.

Bring the whole thing to a simmer. Give it one good stir to make sure everything is friendly. Slap the lid on, turn the heat down to low, and let cook for a good 4 hours. You want to maintain a low simmer the whole time.

When the ribs are falling-apart tender and the aroma is so overwhelming you're afraid you may just break down and eat the whole thing right out of the pot, use tongs to pull the ribs out and arrange on a platter.

If you want, you can thicken up the incredibly rich and flavorful juices in the pot with a little guar or xanthan, but I don't. Pour the juices over the ribs and serve.

Yield: 4 servings

Buffalo Ribs

This super-easy rib recipe is great for winter, when smoking food on the grill is less than appealing. I've called for a half slab in these three sparerib recipes: That's enough to feed three or four people, unless they're the high school football team. But feel free to double these recipes and use a full slab.

2 pounds (900 g) pork spareribs (half a slab)

Salt and ground black pepper

Buffalo Sauce (page 55), for serving

½ cup Blue Cheese Dip With Caramelized Shallots (page 55) or your favorite blue cheese dressing

Per serving: 764 calories; 72g fat (84.9% calories from fat); 26g protein; 3g carbohydrate, 0g dietary fiber

So simple! Preheat the oven to 350°F (180°C, or gas mark 4).

Sprinkle your ribs all over with salt and pepper and lay them in a roasting pan. Roast for about 2 hours, turning the rack over once or twice if you think of it. The timing will depend on how meaty your ribs are; you want the meat starting to pull away from the bone when they're done.

When they're tender, pull 'em out and let them cool for 5 minutes.

Cut the ribs apart; I like my kitchen shears for this task. Put them in a bowl and pour the Buffalo Sauce over them. Now use tongs to toss them in the sauce. Serve with the Blue Cheese Dip and plenty of napkins.

Yield: 2 servings

Buffalo Pork Salad-y Casserole-y Thing

I had leftover Buffalo ribs from the previous recipe; this is what I did with 'em. It's super!

½ a head of cauliflower

6 ounces (170 g) cooked pork ribs

½ cup (60 g) diced celery

¼ cup (40 g) diced red onion

¼ cup (60 ml) Buffalo Sauce (page 55)

⅓ cup (80 g) Blue Cheese Dip With Caramelized Shallots (page 55) or your favorite blue cheese dressing

Per serving: 379 calories; 30g fat (70.9% calories from fat); 19g protein; 9g carbohydrate; 3g dietary fiber

Trim the cauliflower and cut into ½-inch (1.3 cm) bits. Put them in a microwave steamer or microwaveable casserole with a lid (or one that you can put a plate on top), add a couple of tablespoons of water, and nuke on High for about 12 minutes; you want your cauliflower tender but not mushy.

Pull the meat off of your leftover ribs and dice it up.

When the microwave beeps, uncover your cauliflower, drain it, and let it cool just a bit. Dump your still-warm cauliflower into a bowl, and add the pork, celery, onion, and Buffalo Sauce. Toss well. Serve topped with Blue Cheese Dip.

Yield: 3 servings

Braised Chorizo and Cabbage
This is based on a recipe for a side dish that I saw in a Spanish cookbook—or, rather, an English cookbook about Spanish cooking. It only had a little chorizo to flavor it. I thought, "How could more chorizo hurt?"

13 ounces (365 g) Spanish-style chorizo or other smoked sausage

½ cup (112 g) butter

2 teaspoons ground coriander

5 cloves of garlic, crushed

½ a head of green cabbage, coarsely chopped

½ cup (120 ml) dry sherry

Per serving: 555 calories; 47g fat (79.3% calories from fat); 20g protein; 8g carbohydrate; 2g dietary fiber

Slice the chorizo in half lengthwise. Lay the two halves flat side down and slice 'em both lengthwise again. (You're making long, skinny quarters.) Now slice across them, making about ½-inch (1.3 cm) bits.

Put the biggest darned skillet you can find over medium heat. Melt a couple of tablespoons (28 g) of the butter and throw in your chorizo bits. Brown them a little. When your chorizo has a touch of gold, add the rest of the butter, plus the coriander and garlic. Let the butter melt and then stir it all up. Add the cabbage and stir it in, using your spatula to turn it all over and really work the chorizo bits through the cabbage. Let it sauté, stirring from time to time, for about 10 minutes.

Add the sherry, stir it in, and cover the pan. Let it all simmer for 20 to 25 minutes.

Uncover and let it simmer for just another few minutes to cook down the liquid a little, then serve.

Yield: 5 servings

Stir-Fried Pork and Cabbage

This recipe is for when you're in the mood for Chinese food. Find the black bean sauce in the Asian section of your grocery store. It does contain a little sugar, but there's not enough of the sauce in the recipe to spike your blood sugar.

14 ounces (390 g) pork shoulder (Pork shoulder steak is perfect.)

½ a head of green cabbage

½ a medium onion

3½ teaspoons (18 g) black bean sauce

1 tablespoon (15 ml) sriracha sauce

1 clove of garlic, minced

1 tablespoon (8 g) grated fresh ginger

¼ cup (56 g) coconut oil or lard

Per serving: 621 calories; 55g fat (78.9% calories from fat); 27g protein; 6g carbohydrate; 1g dietary fiber

Cut the pork into thin strips about 1 inch (2.5 cm) long. Shred the cabbage about ¼ inch (6 mm) thick and slice the onion thinly, the long way.

In a small bowl, stir together the black bean sauce, sriracha, garlic, and grated ginger. Have this ready by the stove.

Put your big, heavy skillet or wok over the highest heat. When it's good and hot, add 2 tablespoons (28 g) of the coconut oil and let it melt.

Throw in the pork and stir-fry it until all the pink is gone. Scoop it out and put it on a clean plate. Put the rest of the oil in the pan and let it heat. Throw in the cabbage and onion and stir-fry till they're just tender-crisp.

Add the pork back to the skillet and pour in the sauce. Toss everything together till it's all good and friendly and then serve.

NOTE: You could add a splash of soy sauce to this at the end if you wanted, but it's not essential.

Yield: 2 servings

Ham and Broccoli Pot Pie with "Corn Bread" Crust

Omigosh. If he hadn't already married me, this would have made That Nice Boy I Married propose. This takes a little work, but it will thrill the whole family—and use up leftover ham.

1 pound (455 g) frozen broccoli cuts (smaller than spears, bigger than chopped)

3 cups (450 g) ham cubes, about ½ inch (1.3 cm)

1 batch Mushroom Sauce (page 59)

1 cup (230 g) sour cream

5 large eggs, divided

1 cup (115 g) shredded cheddar cheese

4 ounces (115 g) provolone cheese, sliced or shredded

¾ cup (84 g) almond meal

2 tablespoons (14 g) coconut flour

2 teaspoons Swerve, or 12 drops liquid stevia

¾ teaspoon baking powder

¼ teaspoon salt

½ cup (120 ml) heavy cream

¼ cup (55 g) butter, melted

Per serving: 601 calories; 48g fat (71.0% calories from fat); 29g protein; 15g carbohydrate; 4g dietary fiber

Put your frozen broccoli in a microwaveable casserole dish or microwave steamer, add a couple of tablespoons (28 ml) of water, and give it just 5 minutes on High.

Preheat the oven to 325°F (170°C, or gas mark 3). Grease a 3-quart (2.8 L) casserole dish or coat with nonstick cooking spray.

Put your ham cubes in it. Drain the broccoli and throw that in, too. Whisk together the Mushroom Sauce, sour cream, and 2 of the eggs. Scrape all this into the casserole and stir till the ham and broccoli are all evenly mixed and coated. Spread the mixture evenly over the bottom of the casserole.

Sprinkle the shredded cheddar evenly over the top and then lay the provolone over that.

In a bowl, combine the almond meal, coconut flour, Swerve, baking powder, and salt. Whisk the dry ingredients together.

Add the remaining 3 eggs, cream, and melted butter and whisk just till everything's well combined. Pour/spoon your batter into the casserole dish, covering the whole thing.

Bake for 45 minutes or until the "corn bread" is golden and pulling away from the sides. Serve!

Yield: 8 servings

149

Pork-and-Egg Stack Thing

Okay, the recipe title is lame, but the dish is not. Yum. These proportions are for one serving, but as you can see, it's easy to make as many servings as you need to, assuming you have the pulled pork and cheese sauce on hand. Which you should—at least sometimes.

¼ cup (60 ml) Mexican-ish Cheese Sauce (page 45)

2 large eggs

2 teaspoons lard

2 ounces (55 g) Tex-Mex Pulled Pork (page 151)

½ an avocado, sliced

Put the Mexican-ish Cheese Sauce in a pan over low heat to warm it up.

Fry the eggs in the lard to your desired degree of doneness. While they're cooking, put your pulled pork on a plate and nuke it for 40 to 45 seconds on 70 percent power to warm it.

Put the fried eggs on top of the pulled pork. Put the avocado slices on top and then spoon the warm cheese sauce over the whole thing. Amazing.

Yield: 1 serving

Per serving: 664 calories; 59g fat (78.7% calories from fat); 26g protein; 10g carbohydrate; 3g dietary fiber

Cajun Hash with Andouille

Andouille is Cajun-style smoked sausage, and it's awfully good. If you can't find it locally and are using another smoked sausage, you might want to increase the amount of Creole seasoning.

¼ of a head of cauliflower, cut into in ½-inch (1.3 cm) chunks (about 4 cups [400 g])

6 ounces (170 g) andouille or smoked sausage

¼ cup (56 g) bacon grease, divided

⅓ cup (55 g) diced onion

¼ cup (38 g) chopped bell pepper (any color)

¼ cup (30 g) diced celery

2 tablespoons (8 g) minced fresh parsley

1 teaspoon Creole seasoning

Trim the cauliflower and cut it into bits about ½ inch (1.3 cm). Put 'em in a microwaveable casserole with a lid or a microwave steamer, add a couple of tablespoons (28 ml) of water, cover, and nuke on High for 8 minutes.

Meanwhile, quarter the sausages lengthwise and then slice about ¼ inch (6 mm) thick. Put your big, heavy skillet over medium heat and melt 2 tablespoons (28 g) of the bacon grease. Throw in the sausage bits and brown them, stirring as needed.

When the sausage is browned, scoop it onto to a plate and keep it by the stove. Throw the onion, bell pepper, celery, and parsley into the skillet, and stir them around in the grease. Let those veggies sauté for a few minutes.

Per serving: 548 calories; 52g fat (85.9% calories from fat); 13g protein; 7g carbohydrate; 2g dietary fiber

(continued on page 151)

Cajun Hash with Andouille
(continued from page 150)

Drain the cauliflower and add it to the skillet, along with the rest of the bacon grease. Stir it all up together and then spread in an even layer in the skillet. Let it cook for about 5 minutes and stir again. Continue this—letting it cook for 5 minutes, then stirring—until the cauliflower starts to get a bit golden. At that point, sprinkle on the Creole seasoning and stir it in, then spread the hash out again, and let it keep browning!

When your hash is a pretty golden color all through, stir in the andouille, let it heat through, and serve.

Yield: 2 servings

Tex-Mex Pulled Pork Around here, pork shoulder goes on sale for as cheap as $1.49 a pound. Throw it in your slow cooker as soon as you get up, leave it all day, and bring the gang home to pulled pork.

4½ pounds (2 kg) pork shoulder roast (picnic or Boston butt)

3 tablespoons (42 g) bacon grease

½ a medium onion, chopped

5 cloves of garlic, crushed

1 can (14 ounces, or 390 g) diced tomatoes

2 chipotle chiles in adobo sauce, minced, plus a couple of teaspoons of the sauce

2 teaspoons dried oregano

1 teaspoon ground cumin

Per serving: 518 calories; 40g fat (69.7% calories from fat); 34g protein; 5g carbohydrate; 1g dietary fiber

In your big, heavy skillet over medium-high heat, brown the pork roast all over in the bacon grease. Take the time to turn it and get all the sides nice and brown.

When it's brown, plop it into a large slow cooker. Put the skillet back on the burner. Add all of the remaining ingredients to the skillet and stir it all around, scraping up all the tasty brown bits on the bottom of the skillet. Pour this over the pork roast.

Slap on the lid, set the cooker to Low, and let the sucker cook for a good 8 to 10 hours.

When the pork is falling-apart-tender, use tongs and a slotted spoon to fish the roast out and put it on a platter. Using forks, shred the pork. Discard the bone and any gooey bits of skin. Stir the meat back into the liquid in the pot. You are now ready to use your pork for all sorts of things!

Yield: 8 servings

Somewhat Indian Lamb Burgers

The ground lamb I can buy locally is nicely speckled with fat—good, grass-fed fat. If you don't have garam masala, you can sub ⅛ teaspoon ground cinnamon.

1 pound (455 g) ground lamb
1 large egg
½ cup (60 g) pork rind crumbs
½ cup (8 g) minced fresh cilantro
2 teaspoons curry powder
½ teaspoon garam masala
½ teaspoon ground cumin
¼ teaspoon cayenne pepper
1 clove of garlic, crushed
Salt and ground black pepper

Just put everything but the salt and pepper in a large bowl and use your clean hands to smoosh it all up really well. Form into 4 patties about ¾ inch (1.9 cm) thick.

Put your big, heavy skillet over medium-low heat and let it get hot. Salt and pepper your burgers, throw them in the pan and give them 6 to 7 minutes per side, depending on how well done you like your lamb; mine was just barely pink in the middle, but not at all dry. Serve right away.

Yield: 4 servings

Per serving: 401 calories; 31g fat (71.4% calories from fat); 27g protein; 1g carbohydrate, 0g dietary fiber

I'm Feeling Mediterranean Lamb Burgers

These generously seasoned lamb burgers feature a creamy, lemony, garlicky sauce. If you don't have dried mint, oregano would do. But get some dried mint for next time.

½ a lemon
½ cup (115 g) sour cream
4 cloves of garlic, crushed, divided
1 scallion, finely minced
⅛ teaspoon salt
1 pound (455 g) ground lamb
2 tablespoons (20 g) minced onion
1½ teaspoons dried mint
1½ teaspoons ground ginger
½ teaspoon salt or Vege-Sal
½ teaspoon ground black pepper

First make your sauce: Zest and juice the half lemon and add both to the sour cream. Add 1 clove of the crushed garlic and the scallion and then stir in the salt. Let this sit and blend flavors while you make the burgers—indeed, you can do this hours in advance.

Put the ground lamb in a mixing bowl. Add the onion, remaining crushed garlic, mint, ginger, salt, and pepper. Use your clean hands to smoosh it all together very well. Form the lamb into 3 burgers about 1 inch (2.5 cm) thick. At this point, you can refrigerate the burgers for a while if you like.

(continued on page 153)

I'm Feeling Mediterranean Lamb Burgers

(continued from page 152)

Per serving: 526 calories; 44g fat (74.9% calories from fat); 27g protein; 6g carbohydrate; 1g dietary fiber

Put your big, heavy skillet over medium-low heat and let it get hot before you add the burgers. Give 'em maybe 5 minutes per side till they are browned. Serve with the sauce.

NOTE: A nice addition to this is would be drain and chop some canned artichoke hearts and heat them in a skillet till they're starting to brown a little around the edges. Top the burgers with the artichokes, then the sauce. But if you don't have any artichoke hearts in the house, no worries.

Yield: 3 servings

Kitchen Sink Greek Lamb Steak
I had a lamb steak, and I had all this other stuff in the fridge, so this is what happened, and it was *amazing*. Lamb chops would work fine, too.

5 tablespoons (75 ml) olive oil, divided

¼ of a small onion, finely diced

4 green or black olives, pitted and chopped

3 or 4 pepperoncini peppers, drained and diced

1 canned artichoke heart, chopped

2 cloves of garlic, minced

2 tablespoons (8 g) minced fresh parsley

½ teaspoon lemon juice

1 pound (455 g) lamb leg steak, ¾ inch (1.9 cm) thick

2 tablespoons (19 g) crumbled feta cheese

Salt and ground black pepper

Per serving: 766 calories; 67g fat (79.1% calories from fat); 34g protein; 6g carbohydrate; 1g dietary fiber

Put your big, heavy skillet over medium-low heat and heat ¼ cup (60 ml) of the oil.

Add the onion to the skillet and after a minute or so add the olives, pepperoncini, artichoke, garlic, and parsley. Sauté the whole thing for about 5 minutes. Stir in the lemon juice, then scoop the veggie mixture out of the skillet, put in on a plate, and let it hang around by the stove.

Add the last tablespoon (15 ml) of olive oil to the skillet and turn the heat up to medium. Season the lamb with salt and pepper on both sides and throw it in. Give it about 5 minutes per side; set the timer. You want it browned on the outside but still pink in the middle. (Not red! Pink.)

When your steak is done, spread the feta crumbles over it, transfer to a platter, and then spoon the vegetable mixture over it. Slice and serve.

NOTE: Lamb chops tend to be hideously expensive. I watch for sales on whole legs of lamb and then have the nice meat counter folks slice them into steaks for me. I stash them in the freezer and pull them out as I need them.

Yield: 2 servings

Seafood

Fish is an interesting proposition for a low-carb, high-fat diet. On the one hand, it's nutritious, versatile, and quick to cook. Also, many people love it. On the other hand, even what we think of as "fatty fishes" are quite low in fat—salmon derives only 28 percent of its calories from fat, and white fishes like cod, flounder, and sole run 8 to 12 percent.

This means that you need to cook fish with plenty of fat, or serve it with a rich sauce, or accompany it with a high-fat side dish or a salad with plenty of oil, or plan for some combination of these. Perhaps this is why nature has seen to it that it is a rare sea creature that is not improved by butter.

If you're a fan of simple steamed shellfish—crab, lobster, shrimp—you'll want at least 3 tablespoons (42 g) of melted butter per 6-ounce (170 g) serving to bring it above 70 percent fat. Consider lemon butter, garlic butter, Old Bay–spiked butter, Creole seasoning–spiked butter, butter mixed with Dijon or spicy mustard, or just plain butter, of course.

Fish with Wine, Lemon, and Olives
I asked That Nice Boy I Married what I should call this recipe, and he said "Excellent Fish," but I thought I'd be a tad more descriptive. You'd be hard-pressed to take more than 10 minutes to make this. I used cod because it was on sale, but any mild white fish will be good this way—sole, flounder, and others like that.

12 ounces (340 g) cod fillet
Salt and ground black pepper
2 tablespoons (28 g) butter
2 tablespoons (28 ml) olive oil
¼ cup (15 g) minced fresh parsley
2 tablespoons (28 ml) dry white wine
½ a lemon
20 kalamata olives, pitted

Per serving: 475 calories; 36g fat (69.7% calories from fat); 31g protein; 5g carbohydrate; trace dietary fiber

Divide the fish into smaller portions, with an eye to thickness; you want to put the thicker pieces in to cook first. Season with salt and pepper on both sides.

You'll want a very nonstick skillet. Put it over medium-low heat and add the butter and olive oil. Swirl them together as the butter melts.

When the fat is hot, lay the thick pieces of fish in it. Set the timer for 2 minutes. When it beeps, turn the fish already in the skillet and add the thinner pieces to the pan. Set the timer for 2 minutes again.

By the time the second 2 minutes is up, the thick pieces should be flaky clear through; remove from the pan and place on plates. The thinner pieces may be done, too, but I like to flip them and give them just a little heat on the other side, so they get just a little gold. Transfer those to the plates, too, and keep the fish warm.

Throw the parsley and wine into the skillet and squeeze in the lemon juice. As that's cooking down a little, add the olives; you want to just warm them through.

When the sauce has reduced a little—after just a minute or two—divide the olives between the plates and then pour the sauce over them. Serve immediately.

NOTES: The butter and olive oil mixture will brown a little. Don't sweat it; it gives the sauce a nice nutty tone.

You can easily double this recipe, but I just figured that most of you don't have a skillet big enough for four servings of fish.

Yield: 2 servings

SEAFOOD

155

Kinda Southern-Fried Catfish

You can use this crumb mixture on many kinds of fish; it's just that That Nice Boy I Married loves catfish.

12 ounces (340 g) catfish fillet (1 large)

1 teaspoon ground black pepper

¾ teaspoon paprika

¾ teaspoon onion powder

¾ teaspoon dry mustard

½ teaspoon garlic powder

½ teaspoon ground cumin

½ teaspoon dried oregano

½ teaspoon dried basil

½ cup (60 g) pork rind crumbs

1 large egg

2 teaspoons water

⅓ cup (75 g) coconut oil or lard, plus more if needed

1 scallion, thinly sliced

2 tablespoons (8 g) minced fresh parsley

Per serving 644 calories; 50g fat (69.9% calories from fat); 45g protein; 4g carbohydrate; 1g dietary fiber

Cut the catfish into 2 servings. Pat the fillets dry with paper towels.

In a small dish, mix together the pepper, paprika, onion powder, dry mustard, garlic powder, cumin, oregano, and basil. Sprinkle both sides of the fish with some of the mixture.

On a rimmed plate, combine the rest of the seasoning mixture with the pork rind crumbs.

On another plate, beat the egg with the water till the texture is pretty even.

Put your big, heavy skillet over medium heat and add the coconut oil. While it heats, dip each fillet in the egg wash, then in the crumb mixture, coating well.

Fry the fish in the coconut oil until crisp and the fish is flaky, maybe 4 minutes per side or so. When the fish is brown and crunchy outside and flaky clear through, transfer to plates. Throw the scallion and parsley into the skillet, sauté for 15 seconds or so, then spoon over the fish, and serve immediately.

NOTE: Feel free to double this if your skillet is big enough! Or you could use two skillets. Or cook it in shifts.

Yield: 2 servings

The Other Fried Catfish

This is similar to the previous fried catfish, except in the ways that it's different. There's some extra spiciness going on here from the hot sauce and less herbal seasoning.

12 ounces (340 g) catfish fillet (1 large)

½ cup (50 g) pecan halves

½ cup (60 g) pork rind crumbs

1 teaspoon Creole seasoning

1 large egg

2 teaspoons hot sauce (Louisiana, Tabasco, Frank's—whatever you have on hand)

1 teaspoon water

¼ cup (56 g) coconut oil or lard, plus more if needed

Per serving: 614 calories; 53g fat (75.1% calories from fat); 33g protein; 6g carbohydrate; 2g dietary fiber

Cut the catfish in 2 servings and pat dry with paper towels.

Run the pecans through your food processor until they're the texture of cornmeal. Add the pork rind crumbs and the Creole seasoning.

On a rimmed plate, beat the egg up with the hot sauce and water.

Put the pork rind crumb/pecan mixture on another plate.

Put your big, heavy skillet over medium heat and add the coconut oil. Let it heat while you dip both sides of the fish first in the egg, then the pork rind crumbs, coating it well.

Add the fish to the hot fat and fry until crisp on both sides, maybe 4 minutes per side. Serve immediately.

NOTE: Feel free to double this if you can fit that much fish in your skillet!

Yield: 2 servings

Buttery Cod with Fennel

This is so simple, so elegant, and so good. I came up with this recipe because I had used a fennel bulb and wanted to do something with those leftover pretty, feathery leaves.

1 pound (455 g) cod fillet

Salt and ground black pepper, or Beautiful World Seasoning (page 51)

½ cup (112 g) butter, divided

3 tablespoons (12 g) chopped fresh fennel tops

Per serving: 397 calories; 32g fat (72% calories from fat); 27g protein; trace carbohydrate; trace dietary fiber

Sprinkle the cod lightly with salt and pepper or Beautiful World Seasoning.

In your most nonstick skillet, melt half of the butter over medium heat. Throw in the cod and give it roughly 3 to 4 minutes per side, depending on the thickness of the fish. You want it to brown lightly and be flaky, but not overcooked. When you turn the cod, sprinkle the snipped fennel fronds over it.

When the fish is flaky, transfer to 3 plates. Melt the rest of the butter in the skillet and pour over the fish and fennel leaves. Serve immediately.

Yield: 3 servings

Pesto Salmon Shirataki
Fast, fancy, filling, and healthful: What more do you want from a recipe?

12 ounces (340 g) salmon fillet

1 tablespoon (15 ml) lemon juice

Salt and ground black pepper

2 tablespoons (28 ml) olive oil

3 packets tofu shirataki

⅓ cup (80 ml) heavy cream

½ cup (130 g) pesto sauce

6 tablespoons (30 g) shredded Parmesan cheese

6 tablespoons (54 g) pine nuts, toasted

Fresh basil leaves, for garnish (optional)

Per serving: 645 calories; 53g fat (72.8% calories from fat); 38g protein; 7g carbohydrate; 1g dietary fiber

I'd use a nonstick skillet for this, but you could use nonstick cooking spray: Rub the salmon fillet with the lemon juice and then season it with salt and pepper. In a nonstick skillet over medium heat, warm the olive oil, then place the salmon skin side down in the skillet, and cover the skillet. Let it cook for about 5 minutes; the total time will depend on the thickness of your fish.

In the meanwhile, snip open the shirataki packets and drain and rinse. Put 'em in a big microwaveable bowl and give them 4 minutes on High.

Go check your fish! Flip it and cook for another minute or two until it's done through.

Re-drain the noodles, and zap 'em again for another couple of minutes. Drain one more time.

Okay, the salmon is done. Transfer it to a plate; peel off and discard the skin. Keep warm.

Add the cream and pesto to the skillet and stir them around, scraping up any yummy brown stuff. When you have a nice sauce, pour it over the shirataki and toss to coat.

Break the salmon into bite-size bits and add to the shirataki. Toss again and then pile onto 3 plates.

Top each serving with shredded Parmesan and toasted pine nuts. Heck, throw in a couple of fresh basil leaves if you have 'em on hand and serve immediately.

Yield: 3 servings

Sautéed Trout with Pecans

This is an amazing and classic sort of treatment for trout. You'll need a good-size skillet to make this for more than two people, though, unless you cook in shifts.

8 ounces (225 g) trout fillet

1 tablespoon (8 g) rice protein powder

½ teaspoon Beautiful World Seasoning (page 51), or ¼ teaspoon each salt and ground black pepper

¼ teaspoon paprika

2 tablespoons (28 g) butter

1 tablespoon (14 g) bacon grease

3 tablespoons (21 g) chopped pecans

1 tablespoon (4 g) chopped fresh parsley

1 teaspoon malt vinegar

Per serving: 434 calories; 33g fat (69.0% calories from fat); 31g protein; 3g carbohydrate; 1g dietary fiber

Lay the trout on a plate or sheet of waxed paper or aluminum foil. In a small dish, stir together the rice protein powder, Beautiful World Seasoning, and paprika and dust the fish all over both sides.

In your big heavy skillet over medium heat, melt 1 tablespoon (14 g) of the butter and all of the bacon grease together, swirling to mix. When the fat is hot, lay the fish in it and sauté until done through, 3 to 4 minutes per side. When the fish is flaky and golden on both sides, transfer to a plate and keep warm.

Add the remaining butter to the skillet and let it melt. Throw in the pecans and parsley and sauté just until the pecans smell toasty. Stir in the vinegar, cook for another 30 seconds or so, and spoon this sauce over the fish. Serve immediately!

NOTE: Malt vinegar is the traditional condiment with British fish and chips. Find it with all the other vinegars at the grocery store.

Yield: 2 servings

SEAFOOD

159

Spicy Baked Shrimp
To serve this as a main dish, consider adding cauli-rice to soak up the spicy butter and oil.

½ cup (112 g) butter

2 tablespoons (28 g) bland coconut oil or lard

1 tablespoon (7 g) smoked paprika

1 tablespoon salt or Vege-Sal, or 2 tablespoons Beautiful World Seasoning (page 51)

2 teaspoons ground black pepper

2 teaspoons cayenne pepper

2 teaspoons ground cumin

2 teaspoons dry mustard

2 teaspoons onion powder

2 teaspoons garlic powder

1 teaspoon dried thyme

1 teaspoon dried oregano

1 pound (455 g) peeled large shrimp, tails on

Preheat the oven to 400°F (200°C, or gas mark 6). Put the butter and oil in a Pyrex roasting dish and slide it into the oven while it heats.

While that's happening, mix together all of the seasonings.

Okay, the butter and oil are melted. Pull the roasting dish out, swirl them together, and then lay the shrimp in the dish.

Sprinkle the seasonings evenly over the whole thing and use a spatula to stir and turn it all till the shrimp are all evenly coated.

Bake for 15 minutes. Serve with lots of napkins!

Yield: 3 servings

Per serving: 547 calories; 43g fat (70.7% calories from fat); 33g protein; 8g carbohydrate; 2g dietary fiber

Salmon Packets in Caraway Butter
This dish is different and interesting and very easy to double should you have company. It doesn't even dirty up a pan.

4 salmon fillets, 4 ounces (115 g) each

½ cup (112 g) butter

1 teaspoon caraway seeds

Salt and ground black pepper

Per serving: 336 calories; 27g fat (72.4% calories from fat); 23g protein; trace carbohydrate; 0g dietary fiber

Preheat the oven to 350°F (180°C, or gas mark 4).

Tear 4 squares of aluminum foil each big enough to make a packet around a salmon fillet. One at a time, lay a salmon fillet, skin down, in the center of a square of foil. Top each with 2 tablespoons (28 g) of butter that's been cut into several bits. Sprinkle ¼ teaspoon of caraway seeds over it and season with salt and pepper. Fold the sides of the foil over the fish and fold down tightly; then roll up the ends, making a tight packet.

(continued on page 161)

Salmon Packets in Caraway Butter

(continued from page 160)

Bake for 20 minutes and then check one for doneness. If needed, give them another 5 to 10 minutes. Serve in the packets.

NOTE: Do yourself a favor and go buy a roll of nonstick aluminum foil. It's astonishing how well it works, and that's helpful for a delicate food like fish.

Yield: 4 servings

Crab Cakes

These come in just under the 70 percent fat mark, so add Remoulade Sauce (page 53)! These are very delicate, so flip them with care. Another egg or a little more mayo might make them more structurally sound, but then they'd be a little less crabby in flavor.

1 clove of garlic, crushed

1 tablespoon (10 g) minced onion

1 tablespoon (8 g) very finely diced celery

3 tablespoons (42 g) mayonnaise

1 large egg

1 teaspoon Old Bay seasoning

⅛ teaspoon salt or Vege-Sal, or ¼ teaspoon Beautiful World Seasoning (page 51)

⅛ teaspoon ground black pepper

1 pound (455 g) lump crabmeat

½ cup (60 g) pork rind crumbs, divided, plus more if needed

¼ cup (60 ml) olive oil

Per serving: 370 calories; 28g fat (68.3% calories from fat); 29g protein; 1g carbohydrate; trace dietary fiber

Put the garlic, onion, celery, mayo, egg, Old Bay, salt, and pepper in a large bowl and combine well. Add the crabmeat and ¼ cup (30 g) of the pork rind crumbs and use clean hands to gently but thoroughly combine.

Form into 4 balls. Spread the remaining crumbs in a thin layer on a plate and place a ball in the middle. Press down gently till it's about 1 inch (2.5 cm) thick. Carefully flip and lightly dust the other side with crumbs. Place it on a plate and repeat with the remaining balls; add a few more crumbs if you need them. Refrigerate the patties for 1 hour or more.

When it's time to cook, put your big, heavy skillet over medium-high heat and add the oil. Let it get hot and then gently add the crab cakes. Brown for about 3 minutes per side. Turn the heat down to low and let them cook for another 6 to 8 minutes. Serve hot.

Yield: 4 servings

Creamed Tuna

This is pure comfort food! Serve this over shirataki or Zoodles (page 95). And you're probably expecting this: It would also make a great omelet filling. Yes, I'm predictable. Don't forget the Swiss cheese!

2 tablespoons (28 g) butter

¼ cup (40 g) minced onion

4 ounces (115 g) mushrooms, chopped

¾ cup (175 ml) beef stock (Chicken or seafood stock would work too.)

10 ounces (280 g) canned light tuna in olive oil

½ cup (120 ml) heavy cream

⅓ cup (80 ml) half-and-half

2 ounces (55 g) cream cheese, cut into small cubes

¼ teaspoon ground black pepper

Salt or Vege-Sal

Guar or xanthan (optional)

¼ cup (25 g) grated Parmesan cheese

Per serving: 538 calories; 42g fat (70.1% calories from fat); 34g protein; 6g carbohydrate; 1g dietary fiber

In a good-size saucepan over medium heat, melt the butter and start sautéing the onion and mushrooms. As I generally do, I start with sliced mushrooms and break them up with the edge of the spatula as they sauté. It's easier than chopping them in advance.

When the vegetables have softened a bit, add the stock and bring to a simmer. Let it simmer for 15 minutes or so.

Drain the tuna a bit—no need to stamp on it to get all the oil out or anything—and add it to the broth. Stir in the cream, half-and-half, and cream cheese. Whisk till the cream cheese melts and you have a creamy sauce.

Whisk in the pepper and season with salt to taste. (You can thicken this a little more with guar or xanthan if you want, but it really doesn't need it.) Top with the Parmesan and serve.

NOTE: Do take the time to look for light, not white, tuna, canned in olive oil, not soybean oil. The Italian brands are often light tuna in olive oil. Olive oil is far more healthful than soybean oil, which is nasty stuff, full of inflammatory omega-6 fats. And light tuna is far less likely to be contaminated with mercury than white tuna.

Yield: 3 servings

Soups

love soup of all kinds. However, only certain varieties of soup are truly high in fat, and these are mostly cream soups, made either with heavy cream or coconut milk. Brothy, vegetable-laden soups are wonderful, and can be low-carb, but they are not usually seriously high in fat. However, the ones in this chapter are.

Here's a word of encouragement: Few cooking habits will reward you more richly than making your own broth. I save all my chicken bones, naked though they may be, in a plastic grocery bag in the freezer and my steak bones in another. When I have enough of either kind

to fill my slow cooker, I dump 'em in, cover them with water, and add a teaspoon or two of salt and a few tablespoons (45 to 60 ml) of vinegar. I then slap on the lid, set it to Low, and let it cook for 2 days. Then I let it cool, strain, toss the bones, and use the broth for soup right away or freeze it for later.

If you must purchase broth, Kitchen Basics brand is notably better than most of the other packaged broths out there. You might dissolve a spoonful or two of unflavored gelatin in the broth to get a more home-style texture, not to mention added nutritional value.

Creamy Chicken Taco Soup

This soup comes first because it's my favorite.

2 quarts (1.9 L) chicken broth

14 ounces (390 g) canned tomatoes with green chiles

½ cup (80 g) diced onion

1 clove of garlic

8 ounces (225 g) boneless, skinless chicken thighs

1 tablespoon (8 g) chili powder

2 tablespoons (14 g) smoked paprika

2 teaspoons ground cumin

½ teaspoon cayenne pepper

8 ounces (225 g) Monterey Jack cheese

4 ounces (115 g) cream cheese

1 cup (235 ml) heavy cream

1 teaspoon chicken bouillon concentrate

Guar or xanthan (optional)

⅓ cup (5 g) chopped fresh cilantro (optional)

In a big saucepan or soup pot, combine the broth, canned tomatoes, onion, and garlic. Bring to a boil and then turn it down and let simmer for 20 to 30 minutes.

In the meanwhile, dice up the chicken; this is easier if it's partly frozen. When the onion is starting to get tender, stir in the chicken, chili powder, paprika, cumin, and cayenne. Let it simmer for another 20 minutes. Shred the Monteray Jack cheese in the meanwhile!

When the chicken is cooked through, bit by bit, whisk in the Monterey Jack. Cut the cream cheese into smallish hunks and whisk those in one at a time, too. When all the cheese is melted in, whisk in the cream and chicken bouillon concentrate. Thicken it a little with the guar or xanthan shaker if you like—I like my soup about the texture of heavy cream.

Serve with a little chopped cilantro on top—or not, if you're a cilantro hater.

Yield: 6 servings

Per serving: 445 calories; 36g fat (72.6% calories from fat); 22g protein; 9g carbohydrate; 1g dietary fiber

Thai-ish Chicken Soup This is inauthentic Thai, but quick and good.

6 cups (1.4 L) chicken broth

2 tablespoons (28 ml) lime juice

2 tablespoons (28 ml) lemon juice

2 tablespoons (28 ml) fish sauce

2 cloves of garlic, crushed

2 teaspoons sriracha sauce, plus more for serving

1½ tablespoons (12 g) grated ginger

6 ounces (170 g) boneless, skinless chicken thighs

2 cans (26 ounces, or 765 ml, total) unsweetened coconut milk

¼ cup (4 g) minced fresh cilantro (optional)

Combine the broth, citrus juices, fish sauce, garlic, sriracha, and ginger in a big saucepan and bring to a simmer. In the meanwhile, dice up the chicken.

When the broth comes to a simmer, stir in the diced chicken. Don't just dump it in and let it sit or it will congeal into a lump at the bottom of the pot. Stir for a minute and then let it simmer for 10 minutes.

Stir in the coconut milk and bring the soup back to a simmer. Serve with cilantro on top if you like it and pass the sriracha for the hot sauce fans.

Yield: 4 servings

Per serving: 466 calories; 42g fat (77.2% calories from fat); 18g protein; 10g carbohydrate; trace dietary fiber

August Night Avocado Soup Creamy and rich, this chilled soup is perfect

for a sultry summer evening. It's almost like liquid guacamole. It's so simple; just be sure to have everything chilled before getting started.

1½ avocados

1 cup (235 ml) chicken broth

½ cup (120 ml) heavy cream

3 tablespoons (45 ml) lime juice

1 clove of garlic

½ teaspoon salt

Hot pepper sauce, for serving

2 tablespoons (2 g) minced cilantro

2 scallions, thinly sliced

Scoop the avocado flesh into your blender and add the chicken broth, cream, lime juice, garlic, and salt. Process till smooth. Check to see if it needs more salt; it will depend on the broth you're using. Pour into smallish cups. Garnish each with a couple of dashes of hot sauce, a sprinkle of cilantro, and a scattering of scallion slices. Serve right away.

NOTE: Do not make this in advance! Avocado browns quickly. Just have everything chilled, and you can throw this together in 5 minutes.

Yield: 4 servings

Per serving: 240 calories; 23g fat (81.1% calories from fat); 4g protein; 8g carbohydrate; 2g dietary fiber

Lobster Bisque

This is so fancy! If you can't afford lobster, you could go with a less-expensive shellfish or with monkfish fillet. Do not, however, use the fake seafood (surimi). It usually has added carbs.

2 tablespoons (28 g) coconut oil

¼ cup (40 g) minced shallot

¼ cup (30 g) minced celery

2 teaspoons curry powder

1 clove of garlic, crushed

4¼ cups (1 L) seafood stock

¼ cup (60 ml) dry white wine

1 tablespoon (16 g) tomato paste

¼ teaspoon paprika

8 ounces (225 g) lobster tails

1¾ cups (410 ml) unsweetened coconut milk

Salt and ground black pepper (or Beautiful World Seasoning, page 51, or Vege-Sal)

Guar or xanthan

1 scallion, minced

Per serving: 645 calories; 55g fat (75.7% calories from fat); 26g protein; 13g carbohydrate; 1g dietary fiber

In a large saucepan over medium-low heat, melt the oil. Throw in the shallot and celery and sauté till they start to soften. Add the curry powder and sauté for another couple of minutes.

Add the garlic, then the seafood stock, wine, tomato paste, and paprika. Bring to a simmer and let the whole thing cook for 20 minutes or so.

Drop in the lobster tails and set a timer for 10 minutes. When the lobster is cooked through, pull out the lobster tails with tongs. Split them, pull out the meat, cut it into bite-size pieces, and throw it back into the pot.

Stir in the coconut milk and heat through. Season with salt and pepper to taste. Use the guar or xanthan shaker to thicken the bisque to the texture of heavy cream. Serve with minced scallion on top.

NOTE: Kitchen Basics makes a good seafood stock; it's quite low-carb, and it comes in 1-liter (1 quart) aseptic cartons. That's what I use.

Yield: 2 servings

Cold and Foggy Night Soup

I mean, how perfect would this rich, warming soup be on a damp, dark night when the chill penetrates clear through to the bones?

5 bacon slices

6 cups (1.4 L) chicken broth

1 medium onion

3 medium zucchini

½ a head of cauliflower (Trim the very bottom stem.)

5 ounces (140 g) blue cheese, crumbled

1 cup (235 ml) heavy cream

¼ cup (15 g) minced fresh parsley

Ground black pepper

Per serving: 387 calories; 31g fat (70.4% calories from fat); 18g protein; 12g carbohydrate; 3g dietary fiber

Chop the bacon into bits and put it in a big, heavy skillet. (Easier still, use your kitchen shears to snip the bacon straight into the skillet.) Put over medium heat and start those bits browning.

While that's happening, start the chicken broth heating in a big saucepan. Stir the bacon bits! Chop the onion and slice the zukes in quarters lengthwise, then in thinnish slices across.

When the bacon is crisp, transfer the bits to a paper towel to drain. Pour off all but a couple of tablespoons (28 ml) of bacon grease from the skillet. (Save the grease you poured off.) Put the zucchini and onion in the bacon grease and start them sautéing.

Whack the cauliflower into bits. Throw the cauliflower into the heating broth. Stir the sautéing veggies!

Okay, your zukes and onion are starting to soften. Throw them into the broth, too. Let all those veggies simmer in the broth till they're good and soft.

The next step will depend on whether you have a stick blender. If you do, you can do this step right in your saucepan. If not, you'll have to use a slotted spoon to scoop all the veggies into a regular blender. If you do this, add a ladle or two of broth, too.

Either way, measure out 3 tablespoons (24 g) of the crumbled blue cheese and reserve it; dump the rest in with the veggies and broth. Add half the bacon bits, too. If you're using a regular blender, run it till the vegetables are pureed and then dump back into the saucepan. Add the cream and the parsley. If you have a stick blender, simply add all but the reserved blue cheese and bacon bits to the pan along with the cream and parsley and use the stick blender to puree everything together right there in the pan.

Let the soup come back to a simmer and then serve hot, with the reserved blue cheese and bacon bits sprinkled on top.

Yield: 5 servings

Curried Coconut Cream of Chicken Soup

Here's another recipe I've adapted several times—it's just so easy and so good.

6 cups (1.4 L) chicken broth

12 ounces (340 g) boneless, skinless chicken thighs

3 tablespoons (19 g) curry powder

2 teaspoons chicken bouillon concentrate

2 tablespoons (28 g) coconut oil

½ cup (46 g) sliced almonds

1¾ cups (410 ml) coconut milk

Guar or xanthan (optional)

Per serving: 414 calories; 36g fat (75.8% calories from fat); 16g protein; 11g carbohydrate; 4g dietary fiber

Put the broth in a big saucepan over medium-high heat and let it start warming as you dice the chicken thighs. When the chicken is in cubes and the broth is getting warm, stir the chicken into the broth. (If you just dump it in, it will sit in the bottom of the pan and congeal back into a big lump.) Stir in the curry powder and bouillon, too.

While that's cooking over medium heat, you melt the coconut oil in a small skillet. Add the almonds and stir them in the oil until they're a nice golden color. Remove from the heat.

Stir the coconut milk into the soup. Let the whole thing cook for another minute or two to heat through. Thicken it a bit with the guar or xanthan shaker, if you like.

Serve hot, with the toasted almonds on top.

NOTE: I admit that 3 tablespoons (19 g) is quite a lot of curry powder; we just happen to like curry a lot. A whole lot. Feel free to cut back on it, if you wish.

Yield: 5 servings

Turkey Sage Chowder This is what I did with my turkey carcass after Thanksgiving.

1 carcass from an approximately
    18-pound (8 kg) turkey
¼ cup (60 ml) cider vinegar
Salt
1 pound (455 g) turnips
1 pound (455 g) cauliflower
2 leeks
6 bacon slices
1 tablespoon (2 g) ground sage
3 cups (420 g) diced cooked turkey
2 cups (475 ml) heavy cream
Ground black pepper
Guar or xanthan (optional)

*Per serving: 289 calories; 21g fat
(64.1% calories from fat); 17g protein;
8g carbohydrate; 2g dietary fiber*

To get turkey broth, you'll need to put your turkey carcass in a really large stockpot or slow cooker, cover it with lots of water, add the vinegar and about a teaspoon of salt, and simmer everything for a good 12 hours or so. Let it cool and strain out the bones. If there's any meat on the bones, that can be part of the 3 cups (420 g) of turkey that you need.

Put the strained broth back in the stockpot and bring it back to a simmer. Let it reduce till you have about 4 quarts (3.8 L); this gives it a stronger flavor.

Peel and dice the turnips into bits no larger than ½ inch (1.3 cm). Chop the cauliflower into bits about the same size. Quarter the leeks lengthwise. Rinse between the layers and then slice the white part thinly. Toss the green tops.

In your big, heavy skillet, fry the bacon until crisp. Remove it from the skillet and reserve. Leave the bacon grease in the skillet.

Throw the turnips and leeks into the bacon grease and sauté till the leeks have softened.

Okay, your broth has reduced to about 4 quarts (38 L). (I keep saying "about"—soup-making is not terribly touchy. A cup more, a cup less, no big deal.) Add the turnips and leeks to the broth, along with all the bacon grease. Add the cauliflower, too, and the sage. Bring the chowder to a simmer and let it cook till the vegetables are soft, 45 minutes to 1 hour.

Stir in the turkey and the heavy cream. Season with salt and pepper to taste. If the broth is still a little frail-flavored, feel free to use chicken bouillon concentrate in place of some or all of the salt. (You know I have to say it: Beautiful World Seasoning would be good here, too.)

Use the guar or xanthan shaker to thicken the chowder to about the texture of heavy cream. Serve with the bacon (remember the bacon?) crumbled over each serving.

Yield: 12 servings

Sippables

As a general rule, I am not a fan of beverages with calories in them, whether those calories are from fat, carbs, or protein. (I make an exception for alcohol. Red wine is too good to pass up.) My usual beverages are tea, both hot and iced, and sparkling water.

However, there is a place for beverages in low-carb, high-fat eating, not for thirst-quenching purposes, but as a quick breakfast or as a snack. If you're long on protein and short on fat for the day, these are a great way to shift your percentages.

You'll notice a predominance of coconut milk in these recipes. I did this partly for the non-dairy folks and partly because of the strong ketogenic benefits of coconut oil. If you're allergic to coconut or just don't like the stuff, I see no reason not to use heavy cream instead. Just keep in mind that it's roughly twice the fat-and-calorie density of coconut milk; I'd mix it with a bit of water, and if you're fat fasting, you'll need to cut the quantity in half.

Coconut-Vanilla Coffee

"Bulletproof Coffee"—coffee with unsalted butter instead of cream—is gaining popularity, but MCT oil is more ketogenic. That Nice Boy I Married *loves* this, claiming it's better than coffee with regular cream.

1 cup (235 ml) hot brewed coffee

¼ cup (60 ml) unsweetened coconut milk

1 tablespoon (15 ml) MCT oil

18 drops liquid stevia (French vanilla flavor)

½ teaspoon vanilla extract

This is simple: Just combine everything in your blender and run until the coconut milk has melted and it's frothy.

Yield: 1 serving

Per serving: 242 calories; 25g fat ***(92.9% calories from fat)****; 1g protein; 3g carbohydrate; trace dietary fiber*

Cococcino

Here's a frosty, sweet coffee drink for all of you who have given up dairy—and, of course, it has no sugar, too. Plus, think of the money you'll save!

1½ cups (355 ml) unsweetened coconut milk, chilled

⅔ cup (160 ml) brewed espresso, cooled

2 tablespoons (30 g) powdered Swerve

20 drops liquid stevia (vanilla, chocolate, hazelnut, or English toffee flavor)

About 10 ice cubes

Put everything but the ice in your blender and turn it on.

Drop in the ice cubes, one at a time, and run till the ice is pulverized. Pour and drink.

NOTE: You could use sugar-free coffee-flavoring syrup in place of the liquid stevia, if you prefer. It is less concentrated than liquid stevia; use to taste.

Yield: 2 servings

Per serving: 340 calories; 36g fat ***(89.9% calories from fat)****; 3g protein; 6g carbohydrate; trace dietary fiber*

Coconut Chai

This spiced, sweetened Indian tea is commonly made with dairy milk, but coconut milk is popular in India as well, so it seemed a natural here.

8 tea bags

4 cups (950 ml) water

½ teaspoon liquid stevia (plain or English toffee flavor)

1 teaspoon ground cinnamon

1 teaspoon ground cardamom

½ teaspoon ground nutmeg

½ teaspoon ground ginger

¼ teaspoon ground cloves

1¾ cups (410 ml) unsweetened coconut milk

Per serving: 101 calories; 10g fat **(84.1% calories from fat)**; *1g protein; 3g carbohydrate; trace dietary fiber*

In a big saucepan, combine everything but the coconut milk and bring to a boil. Turn off the burner and let it all steep as it cools.

Strain through a fine-mesh strainer or let the spices settle to the bottom and pour off the tea as carefully as possible, leaving the powdery stuff behind.

Stir in the coconut milk. Store in the fridge and serve either hot or cold.

NOTES: Once again, the testers had ideas!

Burma says she likes this with the thinner coconut milk from the carton. She also liked it with a touch more stevia.

Valerie used 2 heaping tablespoons (about 18 g) of xylitol instead of the stevia and heavy cream instead of the coconut milk. She says she prefers to make the tea ahead of time and keep it in the fridge, then add the cream just before serving. She suggests 1 cup (235 ml) chai to ¼ cup (60 ml) cream.

Yield: 8 servings

Almond Cocoa
This is rich and delicious and super-filling. Do not expect to drink this in addition to breakfast: This *is* breakfast!

1¾ cups (410 ml) unsweetened coconut milk

½ cup (120 ml) water

¼ cup (65 g) almond butter

1 ounce (28 g) bitter baking chocolate

¼ teaspoon liquid stevia (chocolate flavor)

⅛ teaspoon almond extract

Put everything in a small saucepan over low heat. Whisk often as you bring it to a simmer. Keep whisking till the almond butter and chocolate are completely melted and blended in. When it's good and hot, pour into cups and serve!

Yield: 2 servings

Per serving: 653 calories; 66g fat ***(84.5% calories from fat)****; 12g protein; 15g carbohydrate; 6g dietary fiber*

Peanut Butter Cup Cocoa
How can you not love this? It's peanut butter cups in a mug.

1¾ cups (410 ml) unsweetened coconut milk

½ cup (120 ml) water

1 ounce (28 g) bitter baking chocolate

¼ cup (65 g) natural peanut butter

¼ teaspoon liquid stevia (English toffee flavor)

Just put everything in a small, heavy saucepan over very low heat and whisk often to mix in the melting chocolate and peanut butter. When it's all blended and heated through, serve.

Yield: 2 servings

Per serving: 631 calories; 62g fat ***(83.8% calories from fat)****; 12g protein; 15g carbohydrate; 4g dietary fiber*

Eric's Butterscotch-Coconut Brew
This beverage was inspired by my husband's childhood passion for Zagnut candy bars. He loves this.

1¾ cups (410 ml) unsweetened coconut milk

¼ cup (60 ml) water

2 teaspoons vanilla extract

¼ teaspoon liquid stevia (English toffee flavor)

¼ teaspoon molasses

Pinch of salt (a teeny pinch!)

Just combine everything in a saucepan, whisk it together, and bring it to a simmer. Pour into mugs and serve. Come to think of it, you could pour the combo into mugs and microwave it instead, if you prefer.

Yield: 2 servings

Per serving: 403 calories; 41g fat ***(89.5% calories from fat)****; 4g protein; 7g carbohydrate; 0g dietary fiber*

Coco-Nog 1
This nog is for those of you who are unafraid of raw eggs. It makes a quick and easy breakfast! (And if you like, you can pasteurize the eggs first; see page 42.)

1¾ cups (410 ml) unsweetened coconut milk, chilled

4 large eggs

24 drops liquid stevia (vanilla flavor)

24 drops liquid stevia (English toffee flavor)

2 pinches of ground nutmeg

Pinch of salt

This is so easy! Just put it all in your blender, run until smooth, and pour into glasses.

Yield: 2 servings

Per serving: 504 calories; 49g fat ***(84% calories from fat)****; 15g protein; 6g carbohydrate; trace dietary fiber*

Coco-Nog 2
For those of you who are nervous about raw eggs, this is really a drinkable coconut custard version of the previous recipe. Serve it with a shot of booze, if you like.

1¾ cups (410 ml) unsweetened coconut milk

3 egg yolks

1 teaspoon vanilla extract

¼ teaspoon liquid stevia (vanilla flavor)

⅛ teaspoon ground nutmeg, plus more for garnish

Pinch of salt

Put everything in a heavy saucepan and whisk it together well. Now put it over low heat. Keep whisking. The price of cooked eggnog is a stiff elbow. Really, you need to whisk it about every 30 to 60 seconds. When it thickens to the point where it will coat a spoon, it's done. Pour it into a jar and refrigerate well.

Serve with an extra dusting of nutmeg.

Yield: 2 servings

Per serving: 484 calories; 49g fat *(88.5% calories from fat); 8g protein; 6g carbohydrate; trace dietary fiber*

Farmer's Soda
This is for those of you who are okay with artificial sweeteners. Burma says this reminds her and her husband, Tom, of the ice cream sodas of their youth! There are loads of flavoring syrups on the market these days, so go crazy experimenting with different flavors.

2 tablespoons (28 ml) sugar-free coffee-flavoring syrup of your choice

¼ cup (60 ml) heavy cream, chilled

1 cup (235 ml) chilled club soda or sparkling water

This is super-simple! Put the syrup and cream in a glass and stir 'em up. Fill with the chilled club soda or sparkling water and serve.

NOTES: This is infinitely variable. How about chocolate syrup and rasp-berry sparkling water? Vanilla syrup and lemon sparkling water? Caramel syrup and coconut sparkling water? Peach syrup and peach-pear sparkling water? La Croix makes a range of yummy flavors to try.

My testers were undecided about whether this was better with more cream or less. Try it this way first and then adjust to your preference.

You can also skip the syrup and sparkling water and use your favorite diet soda. I just don't like soda.

Yield: 1 serving

Per serving: 205 calories; 22g fat *(94.5% calories from fat); 1g protein; 2g carbohydrate; 0g dietary fiber*

Sweets

As always, I approach the dessert chapter with mixed feelings—I think it's best to get out of the dessert habit, but I know that for many people, the knowledge that they can have something sweet now and then is what lets them keep going.

Truly, except when I'm working on a book, I rarely make desserts. We'll have one or two sugar-free mini peanut butter cups a day (it is my considered opinion that Reese's sugar-free peanut butter cups are superior) or a square or two of 85 percent dark chocolate, but that's about it. We reserve desserts mostly for special occasions.

Still, all of these are delicious, nutritious, filling, and won't mess up your blood sugar, and a few of them are actually perfect for fat fasting.

Strawberries and Cream Cheese This makes a super-easy casual dessert.

For a nice variation, use lemon drop–flavor liquid stevia and orange extract.

8 ounces (225 g) cream cheese, softened

3 tablespoons (45 ml) heavy cream

1 teaspoon vanilla extract

¼ teaspoon liquid stevia (vanilla flavor)

1 pound (455 g) strawberries

Using your electric mixer, whip everything but the strawberries until fluffy. Pile it into a bowl, preferably the bowl of a chip and dip platter.

Surround the bowl of cream cheese dip with the strawberries and serve.

Yield: 6 servings

Per serving: 181 calories; 16g fat (78.7% calories from fat); 3g protein; 6g carbohydrate; 2g dietary fiber

Cannoli Pudding This pudding is all of the rich goodness of a cannoli except without

the pastry shell. It's so creamy and delicious!

1 cup (240 g) mascarpone cheese

1 cup (250 g) full-fat ricotta cheese

36 drops liquid stevia (vanilla flavor)

1 tablespoon (15 ml) lemon juice

¼ teaspoon orange extract

½ teaspoon vanilla extract

2 tablespoons (15 g) raw, unsalted, shelled pistachio nuts

¼ ounce (7 g) 85% dark chocolate

This is easy! Put both cheeses, the stevia, lemon juice, orange extract, and vanilla extract in a medium-size bowl and whip the whole thing with your electric mixer for 3 to 4 minutes until it's light and fluffy. Spoon into little dishes; the servings are small because it's so rich. At this point, you can refrigerate the pudding for several hours if you like.

Sometime before serving, preheat the oven to 350°F (180°C, or gas mark 4). Spread the pistachios on a small baking sheet and bake for 6 to 7 minutes. Chop them medium-fine. Again, you can do this ahead of time if you like.

Just before serving, grate the chocolate over the individual servings of pudding—I use my Microplane grater, and it works perfectly. (If all you have is a box grater, grate the chocolate onto a sheet of waxed paper and then transfer to the puddings.) Top each with chopped pistachios and serve.

Yield: 4 servings

Per serving: 271 calories; 24g fat (78.5% calories from fat); 9g protein; 5g carbohydrate; 1g dietary fiber

Cocoa-Peanut Porkies Redux

Yes, these are pork rind cookie bars, and no, I am not crazy. They are sensational. Oh, and since they're no-bake, they're quick and easy, too.

4 ounces (115 g) bitter baking chocolate

½ cup (130 g) natural peanut butter

¼ cup (30 g) powdered erythritol

3 tablespoons (42 g) coconut oil

3½ ounces (100 g) pork rinds (This is an average-size bag.)

⅓ teaspoon liquid stevia (vanilla flavor; I know, ⅓ teaspoon is a little awkward, but you can put in ¼ teaspoon and then eyeball about another half of that, right?)

Per serving: 89 calories; 8g fat (73.6% calories from fat); 4g protein; 2g carbohydrate; 1g dietary fiber

Grease an 8-inch (20 cm) square pan or coat with nonstick cooking spray.

Put the chocolate, peanut butter, erythritol, and coconut oil in a microwaveable bowl. Nuke on High for 1 minute.

In the meanwhile, stick a hole in the bag of pork rinds to let the air out. Smash it with your fists, breaking the pork rinds up into bits somewhere between ¼ and ½ inch (6 mm and 1.3 cm). Open the bag the rest of the way and dump the smashed pork rinds into a big bowl.

When the microwave beeps, pull out the bowl and stir. The stuff will not be completely melted, so give it another minute on High.

Stir the chocolate–peanut butter mixture up again. If it's not all melted, give it one more minute. Once it is all melted, stir in the liquid stevia.

Pour the chocolate–peanut butter mixture over the pork rinds and use a rubber scraper to stir it in until the pork rind bits are all evenly coated. Turn the mixture into the prepared pan and press out into an even layer.

Chill for a few hours and then cut into bars. Store in the fridge.

NOTES: I first devised this recipe using sugar-free chocolate chips. But they can be hard to find—I have to special-order them—so I thought I'd come up with a version using bitter baking chocolate.

You'll notice I used powdered erythritol instead of Swerve in this recipe. There's no particular reason for that. You can use powdered Swerve instead, if that's what you have in the house.

Bonus idea: Press this into a pie plate and refrigerate, and you'll have a great crust. Fill it with sugar-free ice cream!

Yield: 25 servings

Chocolate-Hazelnut Spread

I've never tried the über-popular Nutella; it hit the market after I stopped eating sugary stuff, so I have no idea how this compares. This is awfully good in its own right, though. I found myself having to make fresh batches to try it in recipes because I ate it up straight off a spoon.

2 cups (270 g) hazelnuts

2½ ounces (70 g) bitter baking chocolate

½ cup (120 g) powdered Swerve

⅛ teaspoon salt

1 teaspoon vanilla extract

½ teaspoon liquid stevia (vanilla flavor)

2 tablespoons (28 g) coconut oil

Per serving: 199 calories; 20g fat (83.5% calories from fat); 4g protein; 5g carbohydrate; 2g dietary fiber

Preheat the oven to 350°F (180°C, or gas mark 4). Spread the hazelnuts in a shallow pan—I used a jelly roll pan—and roast for 15 minutes. Pull the nuts out of the oven and let them cool.

When you can handle the hazelnuts, roll them briskly between your palms or use your palms to roll them on the pan. Most of the brown skin should flake right off. The more of it you get off, the smoother and better-flavored your spread will be.

When you've got the skins off the hazelnuts, put them in your food processor with the S-blade in place. Let it run while you melt the chocolate. I do this in the microwave, but you can do it on the stovetop, if you prefer. When the hazelnuts have been ground to nut butter, scrape the melted chocolate into the food processor and add all the other ingredients. Process, stopping to scrape down the sides occasionally, until you have a well-blended spread. Scrape into a clean jar and store in the fridge.

Yield: 2 cups (592 g), or 12 servings

Chocolate-Hazelnut Cookies

Wow. These are outstanding and will definitely make your official Christmas cookie list. Okay, I admit it, these aren't quite high enough on fat, but they were just too good to leave out. If you're starting with a block of chocolate, the easiest way to chop it up is to run it through your food processor.

½ cup (68 g) hazelnuts

1½ cups (168 g) almond meal

1 cup (128 g) vanilla whey protein powder

⅓ cup (27 g) unsweetened cocoa powder

1 teaspoon baking soda

1 teaspoon salt

1 cup (112 g) butter, softened

¾ cup (180 g) granular erythritol

¼ cup (80 g) sugar-free imitation honey

½ teaspoon molasses

½ teaspoon liquid stevia (English toffee flavor)

2 large eggs

2 tablespoons (28 ml) vanilla extract

⅔ cup (197 g) Chocolate-Hazelnut Spread (page 179)

1 cup (175 g) sugar-free chocolate chips (or sugar-free dark chocolate, chopped into chip-size bits)

Per cookie: 256 calories; 19g fat (63.8% calories from fat); 13g protein; 11g carbohydrate; 6g dietary fiber

Preheat the oven to 350°F (180°C, or gas mark 4). Line 2 cookie sheets with baking parchment.

Spread the hazelnuts in a shallow baking pan and roast for 10 to 12 minutes. Pull them out and let them cool.

In a medium bowl, combine the almond meal, vanilla whey protein, cocoa powder, baking soda, and salt. Stir them together till everything is evenly distributed.

In a larger bowl, using an electric mixer, beat the butter until creamy and fluffy.

Add the erythritol, sugar-free imitation honey, molasses, and liquid stevia to the mixer bowl and continue beating, scraping down the sides of the bowl often until they're completely incorporated.

One at a time, beat in the eggs, making sure the first is incorporated before you add the second. Add the vanilla and chocolate-hazelnut spread and beat them in well. Turn off the mixer.

Before you add the dry ingredients, let's deal with the hazelnuts since they're cool by now. Roll them between your palms till most of the skins flake off. Now chop them to a medium consistency.

Now, back to the mixer! Start beating in the dry ingredients in 3 or 4 additions, again, scraping down the sides of the bowl often. When all the dry ingredients are in, beat in the chocolate chips and the hazelnuts.

Scoop onto the parchment-lined sheets; I use a 2-tablespoon (28 ml) cookie scoop. (This looks like a little ice cream scoop and is a very useful item if you make many cookies.)

Bake for 12 to 14 minutes. Let them cool for a minute or two on the sheets before transferring to wire racks to finish cooling.

Yield: 24 cookies

Flourless Chocolate-Hazelnut Cake
See? You really, really need to make some of the Chocolate-Hazelnut Spread on page 179.

8 large eggs

1 batch Chocolate-Hazelnut Spread (page 179)

Per serving: 182 calories; 17g fat (80% calories from fat); 5g protein; 4g carbohydrate; 2g dietary fiber

Preheat the oven to 350°F (180°C, or gas mark 4). Cut a circle of baking parchment to fit the bottom of a 9- to 10-inch (23 to 25.5 cm) springform pan. Line the bottom of the pan with the parchment and grease the sides or spray with nonstick cooking spray.

Break all the eggs into a large bowl and use an electric mixer to beat them for 10 minutes. Yes, 10 minutes, so set the oven timer. This is easier if you have a stand mixer.

Warm the Chocolate-Hazelnut Spread till it's runny. I do this in the microwave, but you could do it on the stovetop in a big saucepan. Remember, you're just warming it till it's softened, not cooking it.

Okay, the timer has beeped, and the eggs have tripled or more in volume. Transfer about 2 cups (475 ml) of them to the bowl or pan with the Chocolate-Hazelnut Spread and use a rubber scraper to fold them in until they're all incorporated. Repeat with another 2 cups (475 ml), again folding until it's all worked in. Then repeat with yet another 2 cups (475 ml).

At this point, you can add the mixture back to the bowl on the stand mixer, along with the remaining beaten eggs, and use the lowest speed to blend only till everything is incorporated.

Scrape the batter into the prepared springform pan and bake for 25 minutes. The cake will be pulling away from the pan at the sides a bit when it's done.

Remove the cake from the oven and let it cool completely in the pan before removing the sides. Cut into wedges to serve.

NOTE: This cake is all about procedure. Do not skimp on whipping the eggs; go the full 10 minutes. And do not try to simply beat the softened spread into the whole batch of eggs without taking the trouble to fold in small quantities—this is what maintains plenty of air bubbles, essential to the final texture.

Yield: 16 servings

Chocolate-Hazelnut Frozen Custard

You'll have to make two recipes to prepare for this, but is it worth it? Wow, is it ever. You'll need an ice cream maker, of course. If you have a big ice cream maker, go ahead and make a double batch!

1 batch Crème Polynesienne (page 184)

½ cup (148 g) Chocolate-Hazelnut Spread (page 179)

Per serving: 398 calories; 40g fat (86.2% calories from fat); 7g protein; 7g carbohydrate; 2g dietary fiber

Bring both ingredients to room temperature, if necessary. Put both ingredients in a blender and run it till the two become one.

Pour the custard mixture into your ice cream maker and freeze according to the instructions that came with your unit.

Consume as soon as it's frozen. I didn't really need to tell you that because it will be nearly impossible to resist. But sugarless ice cream of any kind tends to freeze rock-hard if you store it. So just eat it!

NOTE: If you do wind up saving some for later, you'll need to let it thaw and soften a little before you eat it.

Yield: 4 servings

Coco-Cocoa Candy

Not only is this delicious candy full of medium-chain triglycerides from the coconut, it's loaded with fiber, too. This and the two recipes following are affectionately known as "fat bombs."

1½ cups (336 g) coconut butter (see page 48)

2 ounces (55 g) bitter chocolate

¼ cup (80 g) sugar-free imitation honey

¼ teaspoon liquid stevia (chocolate flavor)

⅛ teaspoon salt

1 tablespoon (15 ml) vanilla extract

Per serving: 65 calories; 6g fat (80.5% calories from fat); 1g protein; 3g carbohydrate; 2g dietary fiber

In a saucepan over very low heat or in the top of a double boiler over hot water, melt the coconut butter and chocolate together. When they're both melted, add the fake honey and stevia and whisk till it's all well combined. Then dissolve the salt in the vanilla extract, add to the pan, and whisk until it's completely incorporated. The texture will change as you whisk in the vanilla, becoming thicker and clumpier.

Grease an 8-inch (20 cm) square pan. Press the mixture into it, creating an even layer. Cut into squares and refrigerate for several hours. You'll need to re-cut the squares when it's chilled, but doing it while the mixture is still soft will make the task considerably tidier.

Store in the fridge. If you transfer this to a snap-top container, put waxed paper between layers.

Yield: 36 servings

Coconut-Maple-Walnut Candy

Here's another "fat bomb" for you. You'll find sugar-free pancake syrup at the grocery store, probably with the regular pancake syrup.

½ cup (50 g) walnuts

1½ cups (336 g) coconut butter (see page 48)

6 tablespoons (85 g) butter, softened

¼ teaspoon liquid stevia (English toffee flavor)

¼ cup (80 g) sugar-free pancake syrup

1 tablespoon (15 ml) vanilla extract

Per serving: 85 calories; 8g fat **(83.9% calories from fat)**; *1g protein; 3g carbohydrate; 2g dietary fiber*

Preheat the oven to 350°F (180°C, or gas mark 4). Spread the walnuts on a shallow baking pan, slide 'em in, and give them 6 minutes.

In the meanwhile, combine everything else in your food processor and run it, scraping down the sides from time to time, until it's all well combined.

Add the toasted walnuts and pulse just until they're chopped to a medium consistency and worked through the mixture.

Grease an 8-inch (20 cm) square pan or spray with nonstick cooking spray. Turn the candy into it and press it out firmly into an even layer. Cut into squares and stick it in the fridge. When it's well chilled, transfer the squares to a snap-top container and store in the refrigerator.

Yield: 36 servings

Coconut-Pecan Candy

Butterscotchy and nutty, this "fat bomb" is just plain good!

½ cup (50 g) pecan halves

1½ cups (336 g) coconut oil

6 tablespoons (85 g) butter, softened

¼ cup (60 g) powdered Swerve

¼ teaspoon liquid stevia (English toffee flavor)

¼ teaspoon molasses

1 tablespoon (15 ml) vanilla extract

Per serving: 84 calories; 8g fat **(85.2% calories from fat)**; *1g protein; 3g carbohydrate; 2g dietary fiber*

Preheat the oven to 350°F (180°C, or gas mark 4). Spread the pecans on a shallow baking pan, slide 'em in, and give them 6 minutes.

In the meanwhile, combine everything else in your food processor and run, scraping down the sides from time to time, until it's all well combined.

Add the toasted pecans and pulse just until they're chopped to a medium consistency and worked through the mixture.

Grease an 8-inch (20 cm) square pan or spray with nonstick cooking spray. Turn the candy into it and press it out firmly into an even layer. Cut into squares and stick it in the fridge. When it's well chilled, transfer the squares to a snap-top container and store in the refrigerator.

Yield: 36 servings

Crème Polynesienne

This is the dairy-free version of the classic crème anglaise; it's a pourable custard sauce. Chill and serve over berries, use as a base for frozen custard, or simply drink as a very rich eggnog—whatever you like.

1¾ cups (410 ml) unsweetened coconut milk

4 egg yolks

36 drops liquid stevia (vanilla flavor)

1 teaspoon vanilla extract

Pinch of salt

Per serving: 249 calories; 25g fat (87.9% calories from fat); 5g protein; 3g carbohydrate; trace dietary fiber

In a double boiler, over hot water and low heat, combine everything, whisking it up well.

Keep whisking, and whisking, and whisking. Yes, you have quite a lot of whisking ahead of you. It will take 20 to 25 minutes for your custard to thicken. This sort of job is one of the reasons I have a television in my kitchen.

When the custard is thick enough to coat a spoon, it's done. Remove from the heat, let it cool, and then chill.

NOTES: A whisk is not the only tool you can use for this. A stick blender works, though you'll get a very foamy custard. You could use a handheld electric mixer, too. For that matter, if you're really diligent, you could use a rubber scraper and stir constantly, making sure you scrape every bit of the bottom of the pan. What you have to do is avoid curdling—getting scrambled egg curds in your custard. I started with my stick blender, then shifted to the rubber scraper as it started to thicken. This way, the foaming subsided by the time my custard was done.

Don't try to speed up the process by increasing the heat; you'll get curdled custard.

I've noted this elsewhere: I now use my small slow cooker as a double boiler, by filling it with hot water, setting it on Low, and setting a stainless steel bowl in the top. This works very well, and I find the curved bottom of the bowl makes it easier to stir thoroughly than the flatter bottom of my traditional double boiler.

Various authoritative cookbooks assure me that you can make crème anglaise without a double boiler if you put it over very low heat. I have not tried this, but if your stove has a simmer burner, you might try it. Just remember that heating too fast will lead to hopelessly lumpy custard.

Yields 2 cups (450 g), or 4 servings

The Easiest Strawberry Ice Cream
It's like magic! You'll need a good, heavy-duty food processor for this; a small, cheap one just won't handle the job.

1 pound (455 g) unsweetened frozen strawberries

4 cups (950 ml) heavy cream

½ teaspoon liquid stevia (vanilla or lemon drop flavor), or as needed

*Per serving: 430 calories; 44g fat **(89.9% calories from fat)**; 3g protein; 8g carbohydrate; 1g dietary fiber*

Throw everything in your food processor and run it until the berries are ground up. Taste and adjust the sweetness, if necessary. Serve immediately.

NOTES: A berry or two may get jammed on a blade early on. Stop the processor, work it loose, and proceed.

This will work with any frozen berries and with frozen peach slices, too. If the fruit is a little flat in flavor, you could add a teaspoon or two of lemon juice.

My testers varied on whether the berry-cream balance was right or needed a few more berries. Valerie used xylitol syrup instead of stevia, while Burma tried DaVinci sugar-free raspberry syrup. Everybody loved it!

Yield: 8 servings

Coconut Flapjacks
These easy, chewy cookie bars are my low-carb, grain-free take on an old English standard. They are homey and irresistible. And thanks to my friend Ailsa Marshall, they are also Englishwoman Approved.

¾ cup (165 g) butter

2 tablespoons (40 g) sugar-free imitation honey

¼ cup (60 g) granular erythritol

1 cup (80 g) shredded coconut

1 cup (112 g) flaxseed meal

¼ teaspoon salt

¼ teaspoon liquid stevia (English toffee flavor)

Per serving: 81 calories; 8g fat (79.4% calories from fat); 2g protein; 3g carbohydrate; 2g dietary fiber

Preheat the oven to 350°F (180°C, or gas mark 4). Line a jelly roll pan with baking parchment.

In a small saucepan over low heat, melt the butter, imitation honey, and erythritol together.

In the meanwhile, add the coconut, flaxseed meal, and salt to a medium bowl and whisk them together.

When the butter mixture is bubbling, whisk in the stevia. Then pour into the coconut-flax mixture and stir till everything is evenly coated.

Turn this soft, sticky dough out onto the parchment-lined baking pan and spread and press it out to cover the whole thing evenly.

Bake for 15 to 18 minutes or until evenly golden. Immediately cut into bars while hot. Leave them in the baking pan till completely cool and then store in a snap-top container.

Yield: 32 servings

In retrospect, Dana Carpender's career seems inevitable: She's been cooking since she had to stand on a step stool to reach the stove. She was also a dangerously sugar-addicted child, eventually stealing from her parents to support her habit, and was in Weight Watchers by age 11. At 19, Dana read her first book on nutrition and recognized herself in a list of symptoms of reactive hypoglycemia. She ditched sugar and white flour, and was dazzled by the near-instantaneous improvement in her physical and mental health. A lifetime nutrition buff was born.

Unfortunately, in the late 80s and early 90s, Dana got sucked into low fat/high carb mania, and whole-grain-and-beaned her way up to a size 20, with nasty energy swings, constant hunger, and borderline high blood pressure. In 1995, she read a nutrition book from the 1950s that stated that obesity had nothing to do with how much one ate, but was rather a carbohydrate intolerance disease. She thought, "What the heck, might as well give it a try." Three days later her clothes were loose, her hunger was gone, and her energy level was through the roof. She never looked back, and has now been low carb for 19 years and counting—a third of her life.

Realizing that this change was permanent, and being a cook at heart, Dana set about creating as varied and satisfying a cuisine as she could with a minimal carb load. And being an enthusiastic, gregarious sort, she started sharing her experience. By 1997 she was writing about it. The upshot is over 2500 recipes published, and more than a million books sold—and she still has ideas left to try!

Dana lives in Bloomington, Indiana with her husband, three dogs, and a cat, all of whom are well and healthily fed.

ACKNOWLEDGMENTS

First of all, my thanks to my recipe testers: Valerie Howells, Jen Hoberer, Burma Powell, Rebecca Jaxon, Tere French Ervin, Kim Yarbrough, Tammera Lowe, Erin Kennedy, Christina Robertson, Maria Vander Vloedt, Soren Schreiber-Katz, Amanda Page, Heather Westerberg, Lisa Gonzalez, Arleen Skidmore, Kathy Allison, Kathryn Hanft, Janis Inman, Sheryl Joyce, Tamara Walker, Debi Channon, Laura Warchol. They are a huge part of the reason this book got done in a reasonably timely fashion, and their feedback is endlessly valuable.

Thanks to Jill Alexander for being patient with me, and not thinking I was crazy when I suggested a specifically high fat cookbook, and to Renae Haines, too, for her patience and help. Thanks, too, to the Fair Winds pub board, who trusted me and my sense of where the low carb community is headed enough to okay this project.

Thanks to Eric Westman for his foreword, for all his invaluable research, for his dedication to the low carb community, and for being a sweetheart of a guy. Also for being unafraid to dance.

To the low carb community at large: You are my proudest alliance. I am honored to be one of you.

And, as always, thanks to my husband, Eric Schmitz. You have no idea how serious I am when I say I couldn't have done it without him.

INDEX